I0160560

PRAISE FOR "KNIGHTS OF THE ORDER"

"Only rarely in Kappa Alpha Order does a chapter or commission undertake the effort needed to document its history. New chapters or commissions are properly focused on growth and success, not their early history. Chapters or commissions of long standing have a significant period of years to recall, document, and distill into a final written history. Theta Commission is both new as a Commission and older as the former Theta Second Chapter. The current leadership under Dewey Wise has afforded the time and resources and been immensely successful in documenting Theta's past and present, no small task. Having served as Executive Director for 18 years, I can count on one hand the chapters that have this kind of documented history today.

Brother Wise has superbly blended the history of Kappa Alpha Order, The Citadel, our early Theta Second Chapter, and our beginnings and present Theta Commission into an intriguing tale for all KAs—not just those from The Citadel or Charleston. The Order is most proud of Dewey's work and we appreciate his extraordinary effort to place this history into the hands of our newest brothers and graduates of The Citadel, so that they may write their own history and continue to enrich this tale for future generations."

— Larry S. Wiese, Executive Director, Kappa Alpha Order

"Thomas Dewey Wise's history of Kappa Alpha Order at The Citadel captures perfectly the facts of the long association and also the moral connection of the two institutions' missions. KAO's founding values include "Excelsior" meaning the constant striving for improvement and higher values. The Citadel's mission since 1842 has been "achieving excellence in the education and development of principled leaders". The compatibility of these goals is a constant exhortation in Wise's excellent work and gives comfort that traditional values are not forgotten in our contemporary society."

— Major General John Grinalds, 18th President, The Citadel

"This is a wonderful book, impressively researched and superbly written, as it documents a piece of significant history of two major southern organizations, the Kappa Alpha Order fraternity and the Citadel (The Military College of South Carolina)."

— Major General Roger Cliff Poole, Interim President, Professor Emeritus, The Citadel

Knights of the Order

A History of Kappa Alpha Order at The Citadel 1883 - 2013

Copyright: © By Thomas Dewey Wise, 2016, All Rights Reserved.
Published By: Fenwick Island Press, 3358 Baldwin Lane, Green Pond, SC 29446
First Published 2013
2016 Edition
Manufactured in the United States of America
ISBN Number: 978-0-9910553-0-2
LCCN: 2013954931
Unless otherwise noted, the photographs of historical cadets and scenes herein are used courtesy of The Citadel Archives & Museum, Charleston, SC.
All images and symbols relating to Kappa Alpha Order are used with permission.
Disclaimer: This book is neither endorsed nor supported financially by The Citadel or Kappa Alpha Order.
Please send errata information to dewey@cusabo.com.

Thomas Dewey Wise   #thomasdeweywise

Front cover: The Kappa Alpha Order Official Coat of Arms, adopted in 1897.

Knights of the Order

Thomas Dewey Wise
B.A., J.D., LL.M,
Historian Emeritus, Theta Commission
Kappa Alpha Order

Brothers Faithful Unto Death

Knights of the Order

FOREWORD

October 15, 2013,

KAPPA ALPHA ORDER
J. Michael Duncan, Former Knight Commander
5 Rogers Court
Pantego, Texas 76013
214-886-1865
mikeduncan1865@gmail.com

J was excited to hear of Brother Dewey Wise's plan to write a history of the Theta Commission. In my opinion, KA is deficient in its recorded history and I'm happy to see the historic events of Theta Commission's birth, preserved for future generations.

As a young KA in Texas, my first memory of a Kappa Alpha Order commission was being taught the basics of the Beta Commission at VMI, during my pledgeship in the fall of 1969. I don't recall the details and didn't really appreciate the concept, other than it was something that happened in Lexington, VA. As I grew older and continued my volunteer service to the Order, I began

Brother J. Michael Duncan

to appreciate the unique contributions that Beta Commission provided to KA, and how the relationship was essential to enhancing KA's Military traditions. The commission is a concept unique to Kappa Alpha in the fraternity world, and National leaders of rival fraternities have told me privately that they're envious because we thought of it first. The Executive Council had been informally exploring the concept of a commission at The Citadel for years, and in 2001 during Knight Commander David Warren's term, we included Military Service Academies as a goal in these discussions. We were hopeful the meeting with General Grinalds in November, 2002 would prove to be successful, but as he has stated, "the timing just wasn't right".

Knights of the Order

When I was elected Knight Commander in 2007, I made the establishment of a commission at The Citadel a high priority. The opportunity to initiate men of high character into the Order was an opportunity I didn't want to pass. By appointing men, such as Robert Varnado, Baron Fain and Don Evans, the stage was set to be successful. Later, I was honored to appoint the actual Theta Commission members, consisting of Colonel James A.W. Rembert, Colonel Myron C. Harrington, Jr., Brigadier General Hugh Banks Tant, III, Julian Victor Brandt, III and Alexander S. Crawford. All of these fine men and the addition of our excellent professional staff, headed by Executive Director Larry S. Wiese and primarily including then Director of Chapter Development Jesse Lyons and Archivist E. Kent McMichael.

This book is an excellent read and tells a story that can be enjoyed by every KA. I want to thank Brother Wise for all of his efforts in making it happen.

Fraternally,

J. Michael Duncan
Knight Commander 2007-2011
Kappa Alpha Order

Introduction

rother Dewey Wise's *Knights of the Order*, a history of The
Citadel's Theta Commission of Kappa Alpha Order, offers
a reader all he might imagine such a history would contain, and more.
Knights of the Order begins with a history of the first 23 years of The
Citadel, 1842 to 1865, followed by a history of the beginnings of Kappa
Alpha Order in 1865. Those who know these two histories will find
new facts to consider. These two brief chapters yield to the relationship
among Robert E. Lee, Kappa Alpha Order and The Citadel, followed by
early manifestations of the Theta Second Chapter of KA at The Citadel
in the later 19th Century.

The book offers a detailed discussion regarding the prohibition of
"secret societies," especially Greek letter fraternities, in military colleges
of various kinds from the 19th Century to today. Citadel cadets a century
ago and earlier seem not to have minded risking
official punishment in order to enjoy fraternities
like Kappa Alpha, Sigma Nu, Sigma Alpha
Epsilon and Alpha Tau Omega while enrolled as
cadets. Virginia Military Institute(VMI) resolved
this problem in 1915 by creating a commission
in place of a chapter of Kappa Alpha Order.
Theirs had been the second chapter of Kappa
Alpha, Beta Chapter. Washington College,
later Washington and Lee, was the site of the
founding of Kappa Alpha in 1865, and theirs
was Alpha Chapter.

Brother James A.W. Rembert

A commission is a title given to an individual or a group with a
mission to accomplish. Commissions in Kappa Alpha Order, first VMI
and the Beta Commission, then The Citadel with the Theta Commission,
then the U. S. Military Academy at West Point with the Sigma Alpha

Commission, have as their primary purpose the selecting, nominating and approving cadets during their senior year, followed by initiating just-graduated cadets as Knights of the Order. The initiation takes place usually on commencement day, an hour or two after the conclusion of commencement exercises. That ensures no undergraduate enrolled as a cadet in a military institute or college or academy will be an initiated member of Kappa Alpha Order, which is the finest of the Greek letter college fraternities, we would say.

Brother Dewey Wise offers records of the problems caused by secret societies on a military college or institute or civilian college campus, and shows the official responses. He is accurate and comprehensive. The detailed accounts of the Theta Second Chapter from 1883 to 1885, then from 1885 to 1890, and finally from 1920 to 1924, record the names and brief biographies of all 62 Citadel men initiated into Kappa Alpha as members of Theta Second Chapter during that 41-year period.

As the author concludes his history of the first three appearances of the Theta Second Chapter, he summarizes the kind of gentlemen selected to be members of Kappa Alpha during the 41 years. Among them were a world-renowned missionary, a college president, a law school dean, several medical doctors, two state legislators, one of whom became a circuit judge, several bankers, college professors, many attorneys, a four star general, a two star general, and many colonels, businessmen and farmers. Four were awarded honorary degrees from The Citadel in later years. Five have windows in Summerall Chapel dedicated in their memory. "These 62 men," the author concludes, "were indeed a noteworthy group, whose achievements set a high bar for the future."

The national office of Kappa Alpha Order in Virginia and we in the Theta Commission in Charleston try to imagine how the author came up with such hard-to-find information scattered widely. The answer is simple: hard work. Senator Wise engaged in research, travels to Mulberry Hill in Lexington, Virginia, telephone calls, meetings and discussions with the descendants of Theta Second members. The research and writing consumed two years of constant devotion to this virtually self-imposed duty that was approved and encouraged by his Theta Brothers.

The second half of his history concerns "The Birth of the Theta Commission," 2008 to the present. Of course he begins before 2008 because he is a historian. In 2008 Knight Commander J. Michael Duncan declared the Theta Commission active in a letter to Larry S. Wiese, Executive Director of KAO, dated October 3, 2008. The first five Theta Commission KAs, Brothers Vic Brandt, Lex Crawford, Myron Harrington, James Rembert and Hugh Tant, were initiated in the Episcopal Church of the Holy Communion in Charleston by our brothers in Beta Gamma Chapter of KA at the College of Charleston. The active Theta Commission was granted its charter at a formal meeting at the Carolina Yacht Club in Charleston on March 27, 2009.

One of his most entertaining biographies of those central to the beginning of the Theta Commission is that of "Batman" Varnedoe. Others the author describes are contributors to, advisors to, and members of the incipient Theta Commission. All are with us today, friends and brothers unto death, including Kappa Alphas of other chapters. The story of the formation of the idea to reconstitute a Kappa Alpha Order commission at The Citadel, the individuals concerned and their devotion to the idea, is a good story. Soon after the commission received its charter the world was made considerably better by receiving into its billions annually a constant stream of newly-minted Knights of the Order aglow with highest ideals of honor, integrity, courtesy, chivalry, admiration of the best ideals of the Old South, and possessing personal faith in our Creator.

Since Citadel commencement day in May 2010 we have initiated annually just-graduated cadets and since 2009 older Citadel graduates, so that now we have 291 Theta Commission KAs.

To respond to the author's kind remarks in his acknowledgements: absolutely, Brother Dewey, your history more than meets what you call the old professor's lofty standards.

James Aldrich Wyman Rembert

Wadmalaw Island
October, 2013

Knights of the Order

Acknowledgements

Writing this history of Theta Chapter/Commission has been a labor of love. I love history and I love the values embodied at The Citadel and Kappa Alpha Order. Shortly after I was appointed the V (Historian) of Theta Commission in 2011, I suggested to our Number I (President) that we collect and preserve the history and documents involved in the creation of the Commission. After all, those were among the prescribed duties of the Chapter Historian. I was generally aware that there had been an earlier Theta chapter, known as Theta Second, but had no idea who was in it or even if it was ever active.

As I began researching Theta's history, I became aware of the names of the earlier Theta members who seemed to be from some of South Carolina's finest families. What I had expected to be a two month effort to minimally comply with my duties as Historian, ultimately became a two year effort to tell the complete, fascinating story of Theta, its distinguished alumni and how it evolved.

The history of mankind is in its simplest form, the history of countless individual lives whose actions collectively shape our society. Each life story is important and significant. Some individuals reach high goals and some drop out along the way, but all are important to the end result. Telling those individual stories is the rewarding and interesting part about writing history.

Needless to say, this work could not have been done without the help of many people. To begin with, our Number I, The Chairman of Theta Commission, Colonel James A.W. Rembert, gave the project his full and complete support. He had an unexpressed confidence that I could get the job done and I hope the result fulfilled his hopes. With Colonel Rembert being a career English Professor

at The Citadel and a former classmate of mine, it placed substantial subconscious pressure on me to do a good job. Brother James, this is for you. I hope it meets your lofty standards.

The folks at Kappa Alpha Order National Administrative Office at Mulberry Hill in Lexington, Va. were gracious hosts, endured my visit there and my later, constant badgering for answers to countless questions. Larry Wiese, Jesse Lyons, Sgt. Major Kent McMichael, their support staff including Anita Snyder, Becky Moore and Katie Robey and various interns were most helpful.

Former Knight Commander J. Michael Duncan provided details of his efforts to establish the Commission in recent years. Knight Commander Duncan has graciously written the Foreword which I appreciate. Councilor C.D. "Bubba" Simmons III, provided other historical details and research assistance.

Likewise, this book could not have been written without the total cooperation of the fine staff of the Daniel Library at The Citadel. Lt. Colonel Elizabeth Connor was my main contact person there. She went above and beyond the call of duty to make available to me various documents and books. Dwight S. Walsh, Jr., Archives and Museum Supervisor and Kevin L. Metzger, head of Graphic Arts and Design led me through the myriad of documents and photographs available on the third floor. Lieutenant Colonel David Goble, the Library Director, could not have been more gracious to me in arranging access.

Major Steve Smith, historian for the Citadel Alumni Association, as well as the full time Tactical Officer for Band Company, labored with me in finding old photographs and translating ancient letters. He also allowed me to quote from a portion of his research on fraternities at The Citadel.

Knights of the Order

I am indebted to Donald Evans for the use of his excellent photographs of the Charter presentation.

Kevin L. Metzger, a talented and creative genius, mentioned above did the formatting and graphics for the book.

One of Charleston's finest historians, Doug Bostick, found in his files, long forgotten evidence that answered critical questions relating to the 1920's era. He graciously made those documents available for this book.

Within the Commission, I "drafted" a small number of brothers to gather biographical information of some of the earlier members. I would like to mention that Brothers Jan Malinowski, Bill Davies, Ron Plunkett, John McAllister and John Chase did exceptionally good jobs. Brother Burton Fowles played a major role in helping me with the final biographical details. He spent many hours online and in various libraries running down data. Since he is newly married, I extend my apologies to his bride.

Major Scott Buchanan, a Political Science Professor at The Citadel and a Commission member, gladly gave me valuable advice on publishing, as he was already a published author himself.

I chose two men, Brother Ron Plunkett and Brother Jesse Lyons to review the final document, one from the standpoint of The Citadel and the other from the standpoint of Kappa Alpha Order. Their suggestions resulted in a much improved product and I appreciate the time and attention they gave the project. Both of these men gave me encouragement along the way when the long hours of research and writing seemed to have no end.

My wife and best friend, Patricia, not only accompanied me to Lexington for research, but suffered through many hours alone

Knights of the Order

when I was busy at the library or on the computer with this project. In simple words, she is truly the wind beneath my wings.

I view this book as only a beginning with the hope that every few years it will be updated with more initiates into Theta Commission. As new historical details emerge about our initiates of the 1880's and 1920's, I hope they will be incorporated in later editions.

Theta Commission is now a permanent part of Kappa Alpha Order. With nearly 300 members, and growing at around 75 new initiates each year, it is here to stay. May it continue to grow and prosper.

Finally, despite the help of many people in producing this book, I take full responsibility for any flaws in the final product.

Thomas Dewey Wise

Fenwick Island

October, 2013

Dedication

*T*his book is dedicated to Philip Bascom Hamer (December 13, 1859-February 13, 1929), the Founder of Theta Chapter, Kappa Alpha Order at The Citadel in October, 1883.

Educated at Wofford College, initiated into Kappa Alpha Order in 1878, Editor of The Magazine of Kappa Alpha Journal, (1883-1885) Knight Commander, 1887-1889.

Scholar, Lawyer, Civic Leader, Journalist, Businessman, Husband and Father.

The Father of Theta Chapter at The Citadel

Knights of the Order

Table of Contents

Foreword: Former Knight Commander J. Michael Duncan
Introduction: Colonel James A.W. Rembert
Acknowledgements: Thomas Dewey Wise
Dedication
Preface

Knights of the Order

Preface

*K*appa Alpha Order is more than just a fraternity, it is a group of men who share the ideals of and seek to live, even in these modern times, by the Chivalric Code of Medieval Knighthood. Those ideals are Bravery, Courage, Honor and Loyalty. They strive to seek justice, protect the weak, help the poor and revere womanhood. Their strength is a strong religious Faith that sustains them.

"Excelsior", meaning constant upward striving to improve one's character and values, is the motto of the modern Knight.

This is the story of the creation, evolution and growth of one chapter of Knights of the Kappa Alpha Order.

The creation of Theta Chapter/Commission, like most worthy endeavors, was not the work of one man, but of many. Each of them is profiled in this book. They are a cast of improbable characters, from a Wofford graduate to a College of Charleston transfer student to a "Batman" to three Charleston social buddies, each playing a critical role. Interwoven into the story is the fierce campus competition between the "Greeks" and the "Barbarians", or "Barbs" as they were known.

In the beginning, the year 1883, a small handful of young Citadel Cadets sought to create a fraternal organization in a hostile military environment. They almost failed, but just when things were the darkest, their ranks were filled again with eager initiates. In all, there were 43 men initiated from 1883-1890. These were not just any men, but they were carefully selected, potential leaders. In the 1920-1924 timeframe, another 19 men were initiated. These 62 Knights not only established a solid foundation for the Order, but each of them went on to significant personal achievement in later life. Until now, these 62 men and their accomplishments had been forgotten in the

dustbin of history. They are all long dead now, but their spirit and contributions to society live on. Each of their stories is told in this book.

The creation of Theta Commission in 2008 came about by what some would call happenstance- others would call it Destiny. Its birth and phenomenal growth some would ascribe to beginners luck, others would see the Hand of Divine Guidance at work. The details of this evolution are set forth herein and the reader can make his/her own judgment of how it happened.

Suffice it to say that Theta Chapter at The Citadel in the 1880's survived at all was a miracle, and that it initiated Cadets in the 1920's was incredibly fortunate. That Theta Commission itself was created at The Citadel in 2008 was the culmination of an almost unbelievable set of coincidences.

Just as the Theta Chapter of the 1880's succeeded by selecting good men, the Theta Commission leadership choices made by those in the 2008 era resulted in the success it has enjoyed to this day.

This is the story of that 130 year saga from 1883-2013.

I.
The Citadel 1842-1865

While it was not formally chartered until 1842, the fact is the birth of The Citadel is inextricably linked with two events occurring in 1822 and 1832. The first event was a potential slave revolt uncovered in Charleston in 1822. The second event was the Nullification Crisis of 1832.

Telemaque, as he was then known, was a slave living in San Domingo, when he was brought to Charleston by his owner, a sea captain, named Vesey. Captain Vesey owned a home in his native city of Charleston, and Telemaque was his personal slave. Telemaque has been described as bright and talented. In 1800, he won a $1,500 lottery ticket and used $600 of its proceeds to purchase his freedom. He became a free black carpenter, and his first name evolved to Denmark, which he combined with the last name of his former master. He practiced his trade, married a number of women, had many children and became an important member of the free black community in Charleston for the next 22 years.

Denmark Vesey, with his intelligence and his physical appearance, was an unquestioned leader of the slave community. His reputation was one of ambition and cruelty. Some dispute Vesey's responsibility for the fomenting of a slave revolt in 1822, but the plan as revealed by loyal slaves was one of horror. It involved the seizure of arms from two community arsenals and the slaughtering of all whites and looting of the town.

With the plot unmasked, Vesey and numerous others were arrested and tried. Vesey and 35 of his co-conspirators were found guilty and executed, even though the revolt never took place and no lives were lost. It was the realization of what could have happened in a city

1

with 14,000 black slaves living among 11,000 whites that forced the authorities to examine their security arrangements.

At the time, community armaments were kept in two arsenals, one located near what is now Marion Square and the other farther up the Charleston "Neck" on Meeting Street Road. The legislature decided to sell the arsenal on Meeting Street Road and use the funds to purchase a former tobacco inspection shed on Marion Square and establish a permanent "municipal guard." Legislation was passed in 1822 entitled, "An Act to Establish a Competent Force to Act as a Municipal Guard for the Protection of the City of Charleston." By 1826, the new facility, ultimately known as The Citadel, located about one mile from the Courthouse at Broad and Meeting Streets, was occupied.

In the late 1820's the facility was referred to as the "State Arsenal." For a short time, regular United States troops manned the facility, but with the Nullification Crisis, the request had been made for the withdrawal of the federal troops and they departed on December 25, 1832. Fears of a slave revolt had not subsided, which required protection of citizens from this internal danger.

The Nullification Crisis brought to the fore a possible external danger to the state. South Carolina, reacting to what it viewed as unconstitutional acts of the national government threatened to secede from the Union. The precipitating factor was the "Tariff of Abominations" of 1828. President Andrew Jackson, in turn, threatened to use military force to enforce the tariff laws and hang any who resisted. Fortunately, cooler heads prevailed and the tariff was repealed.

Both these concerns made the state acutely aware of its need for a permanent, trained militia force. Governor John P. Richardson originated the idea of the two public arsenals of the state being converted to military schools. Accordingly, the legislature made provision for

two arsenals/ schools, one (The Arsenal) in Columbia, the other (The Citadel) in Charleston. Collectively, they were known as the South Carolina Military Academy. General David F. Jamison of Orangeburg, Chairman of the House of Representatives Military Committee, introduced the legislation. General Jamison saw to it that the legislation gave broad and sweeping powers to a Board of Visitors to implement the intent of the Governor and the Legislature in creating this school. The education component was modeled after the Virginia Military Institute. Since the primary job of the occupants of these two facilities was to guard the arms, powder and military supplies it became state policy to provide them with military training and education in return for their services.

Thus, the date that the legislation was passed, December 20, 1842, became the birthday of The Citadel.

CITADEL ACADEMY, 1843.

Courtesy: The Citadel Archives & Museum, Charleston, SC

The next day, December 21, 1842, the Governor appointed five men to constitute the first Board of Visitors.[1] General James Jones was the first chairman. General David F. Jamison became one of the original five members of the Board of Visitors. He would serve for 22 years, until his death in 1864, as a member of the Board. In that

3

capacity, he guarded the infant school from legislators who were intent on eliminating it. But, equally important, he helped mold the new institution in its formative years.

Grave of Gen. David F. Jamison, Presbyterian Cemetery, Orangeburg, SC. Authors Collection.

The leaders of South Carolina who gave birth to the South Carolina Military Academy were men of wisdom and foresight. They recognized the need to instill in young men, responsibility as well as patriotism. They also knew that those traits did not reside exclusively with the well to do. They believed that bright young men of good character deserved a chance at a quality education that their parents could not otherwise afford. So, they devised a path to success if those youths were willing to work for it. Establishing a category of "beneficiary" cadets will surely rank as one of the most enlightened educational models of the 19th or any other century.

General David F. Jamison, in addition to being a long serving legislator, was both an attorney and an author. He was chosen as the President of the Secession Convention of 1860 and affixed his signature to that document. He was a man of letters whose best friend was the noted author, William Gilmore Simms. When Jamison died unexpectedly of yellow fever in 1864, Simms was named as his replacement on

the Board. Jamison was buried in a common, unmarked grave at the Presbyterian Cemetery in Orangeburg, S.C. Finally, in 1894, friends collected funds to erect this small monument of South Carolina granite in his honor. The Citadel had no better friend or guiding star in its formative years than David F. Jamison.[2]

Two categories of cadets were admitted in that first class at the South Carolina Military Academy selected on February 24, 1843. The first category was "beneficiary" or "State" cadets.

The beneficiary cadets were selected by competitive examination from the 29 Judicial Districts across the state and were provided a free education in return for military service in guarding state property. They signed up for four years of service and were usually recommended by public school officials. The criteria for their selection were academic qualifications, good moral character and fitness for military service. Beneficiary cadets were usually boys from poorer families who showed aptitude and a strong desire for an education.

The other category of cadets were the "pay" students, also allocated from the judicial districts. While these young men received the same training and education, their families paid the State to educate their sons. These fees were fixed initially at $200.00 per year (raised in 1861 to $240.00). The "pay" cadets could resign from the school at any time as they had no obligation to the state.

Once admitted, the Regulations explicitly provided there was to be no distinction between the two types of cadets, and rank and other privileges were to be awarded on merit alone. This regulation was another enlightened approach that not only leveled the playing field, but logically made achievement the goal of all cadets. The first class enrolled in 1843 was authorized 54 beneficiary cadets and 54 pay cadets.

Knights of the Order

Between 1842 and 1860, The Citadel grew slowly but steadily in numbers and prestige. Cadets spent their freshman year undergoing training at The Arsenal in Columbia, transferring to The Citadel for the remaining three years. The Board of Visitors as well as the Superintendent and faculty were composed of wise and competent men who guided the institution through its infancy. With the advent of the War Between the States, its graduates proved themselves leaders and loyal to their state. They were there at the beginning and at the end.

From 1843 to 1864, there were 1,476 pay and 692 beneficiary cadets admitted for a total of 2,168.[3] Of those:

	Pay	**Beneficiary**
Failed to report and rejected	239	90
Honorably discharged	627	213
Discharged for Deficiency	163	115
Dismissed for Misconduct	198	102
Died	9	7
Graduated	**121**	**119**
Remaining at Academy, Dec. 1864	119	46

Thus, only 11% of all those admitted, graduated. Of the pay cadets, only 8% graduated. The beneficiary cadets had a graduation rate of 17%, or twice that of the pay cadets. These statistics demonstrate that the Academy was a rigorous place both academically and militarily. One would think that the pay cadets, coming from well- to- do families had been exposed to a better preparatory education prior to arriving. Whatever academic shortfalls the beneficiary cadets arrived with, they apparently made up for in determination and desire to succeed after joining the Corps.

The Citadel 1842 - 1865

Citadel Academy — 1850
Courtesy: The Citadel Archives & Museum, Charleston, SC

Up to December, 1864 there were a total of 240 graduates of the South Carolina Military Academy. The 1865 Class of 18 members did not graduate because the Citadel was closed and occupied by Federal forces in February, 1865. However these 18 were later given "honorary degrees", thus making the total of graduates from 1843 to the closing of The Citadel in 1865, 258. Of the 240 living graduates, 209 served in the Confederate forces.

The graduates who did not serve were primarily ministers, physicians and civilian engineers. These Citadel men paid a high price during the War against Southern Independence. Battle deaths were 36 with 13 others dying of other causes, such as disease. Another 29 were wounded. Thus, over 37% of those serving lost their lives or were wounded during the course of the war.

There were also a number of cadets who resigned from the Academy prior to graduation to serve in the Confederate forces. Many of those also lost their lives.

As noted earlier, the cadets remaining at both the Arsenal and The

Citadel also saw action as a unit called the "Battalion of State Cadets". They suffered at least 31 deaths from enemy fire. This battalion (now the Corps of Cadets composed of five battalions) earned a total of nine battle streamers during the course of the war. These were earned for "significant participation in a battle of historical importance." The Citadel is the only educational institution in America to be authorized more than one battle streamer. Virginia Military Institute, Florida State University, The College of William & Mary and the University of Hawaii ROTC units are authorized one each.

By February, 1865, Charleston was ravaged and occupied by Union forces. The Citadel itself was confiscated and used to house Federal troops and the school was closed. In Columbia, The Arsenal had been burned to the ground by General William T. Sherman's troops and was never re-opened. Unfortunately, important records from the Citadel had been sent to the Arsenal for safekeeping earlier. All these records were lost to history in the ensuing fire.

By May, 1865, hostilities were ending when Governor McGrath ordered the furloughing of the Arsenal cadets. There were about 265 cadets still on duty. The Battalion colors, which had seen many battles, were entrusted to Captain John Peyre Thomas, then Superintendent of the Arsenal. This was the same flag given to The Citadel Corps of Cadets by the Washington Light Infantry in 1857.

The Citadel 1842 - 1865

The Citadel under Federal occupation. Note "U.S" insignia on gate. Courtesy: The Citadel Archives & Museum, Charleston, SC.

Endnotes

1.Thomas, p.33. These men were James Jones, David F. Jamison, W.J. Hanna, Daniel Wallace, J. H. Means.

2.Thomas, p.166-175. See Resolution passed by the Board of Visitors on Gen. Jamison's death.

3.Thomas, p. 177

Knights of the Order

II.
Kappa Alpha Order:
The Beginning - 1865

*A*s the War against Southern Independence ground to a halt in the spring of 1865, one of the most devastated areas outside the Deep South was the Shenandoah Valley area of Virginia. Armies on both sides had marched up and down the valley, leaving a trail of death and destruction.

Lexington, located near the southern entrance of the valley was a sleepy town of less than 2,200 souls when the war began. It was the home of two prominent educational institutions. Both the Virginia Military Institute founded in 1839 and small Washington College founded in 1749 were located there. Their campuses adjoined each other in the hills of Lexington.

Washington College was named after the first President who contributed a substantial sum to the college shortly before his death. By the summer of 1865, the future of Washington College looked bleak. The school had received severe damage during the war and even though it remained open, it had no money and no President. Its 40 young men and four professors constituted the entire school.

The school's Board of Trustees met in August, 1865 and one member suggested they offer the Presidency to General Robert E. Lee. Lee, was, of course, a controversial figure. He may have been venerated in the South, but many in the North wanted to put him on trial for treason. After all, in the late war, he had led the Army of Northern Virginia and fought for his state under the Confederate flag.

On the other hand, Lee was unemployed and his name and reputation alone would guarantee the enrollment of many young men wanting to come and study at the institution. No doubt, Lee could have chosen a more lucrative use of his time. A speaking tour on the lecture circuit would probably have assured him a comfortable living. The Trustees of Washington College no doubt thought it was a long shot for Lee to accept their offer.

If so, they did not know Robert E. Lee. Had fame and fortune been his goal, he would have accepted the command of all the Union armies that had been offered to him prior to the war. Placing personal honor and his loyalty to his home state of Virginia above all else, he declined the offer. That choice also cost him the magnificent estate of Arlington Plantation inherited by his wife. Shortly after the war began, the Federals seized the estate and began using it as a burial ground. It is now Arlington National Cemetery.

Lee had another connection to the small college in Lexington. His wife, Mary Anna Custis Lee, was the daughter of George Washington Parke Custis, step-grandson and adopted son of President Washington. Lee's oldest son, George Washington Custis Lee, known as "Custis", was named for his grandfather and would, upon General Lee's death, succeed him as President of Washington and Lee College, serving from 1871 to 1897.

So, maybe the Board of Trustees really knew what they were doing when the offer was made to Lee. Maybe they knew that Lee could not resist the opportunity to help educate and influence a new generation of young southern men. Perhaps they understood, that being a humble man, not given to avarice, Lee would accept the paltry sum of $1,500 per year and living quarters, to devote his full time to the Presidency of the College.

At any rate, Lee accepted and said in his letter to the Board that, *"I think it is the duty of every citizen, in the present condition of the country, to do all in his power to aid in the restoration of peace and harmony."*

Lee arrived in Lexington on August 18, 1865 to prepare to take up his position as President of Washington College. Prior to his inauguration, he chose to stay four nights at the home of Samuel Reid, a college trustee and old family friend. Reid had inherited a fine home on the outskirts of Lexington, known as Mulberry Hill. It is both fortuitous and symbolic that this same home and property is now the National Administrative Office of Kappa Alpha Order.

National Administrative Office of Kappa Alpha Order.

Knights of the Order

III.
THE FOUNDING OF
KAPPA ALPHA ORDER - 1865

*T*he story of the founding of Kappa Alpha Order is best told by the Order's official history recorded in *The Varlet* of the Kappa Alpha Order. Twelfth Edition, 2012, reprinted here with permission.

The Founders

James Ward Wood was born on December 26, 1845, in rural Hardy County, Virginia (now West Virginia). He was the fifth generation of Woods to farm the land near Lost River and his grandson Bill Wood, (who continues his KA legacy as an Alpha Chapter initiate) occupies the family land and the Woodlawn home today. Wood was apparently studying law when his part of Virginia entered the Civil War. He was blessed with a fantastic home library which was wide and varied. While his education was not formal as we know today, he had a rich and broad base of learning. This was accomplished by his intense reading and study of all types of literature. As a young man, Wood was very dignified and deferential, engaging and friendly. In 1864, Wood joined the Company F of the 7th Virginia Cavalry. While home on leave in 1865, Wood suffered a pistol wound to his foot that ended his service. He spent that summer recuperating from that wound, sometimes visiting the local country store which served as the center for community activities. There he met a man (an Odd Fellow and a Mason) who, throughout the summer of 1865, fascinated Wood with tales of "the esoteric" and of secret societies. Partly from this encounter, but mostly from a book on Freemasonry given to Wood by his Uncle Frank in 1861, he became intrigued by the concept of lifetime brotherhood, anchored by genuine fellowship among friends.

It was, in part, Lee's acceptance of the presidency of Washington College, and a new job as the head master of the Ann Smith Academy for girls that caused

the well-respected Reverend John A. Scott to move his family to Lexington in 1865. Rev. Scott's family had once lived in Hardy County and was intimate with the Woods for two generations. Wood's father recognized his son's natural intellect and high moral character and sought to formalize his education. He also believed that his son would profit under the influence of the Rev. Scott, a Presbyterian minister esteemed throughout Virginia.

Wood made his way to Lexington and arrived on campus on October 10, 1865. He wrote home several days later, advising his brother that he "lodged in the College ... in Room No. 4 of 'Paradise'" (the name given by the students residing there to the building now known as Robinson Hall). Wood quickly became a member of the esteemed Washington Literary Society and was known for his poems and essays that appeared in the campus paper. He soon became known as the "College Bard" on campus. He also was known to enrich his conversations by quoting Biblical scripture and lines from literature. He was impressed with phrases that he had not heard before and sounded unique. Sometime before the close of the spring semester, Wood received permission from his father to leave campus and board about a mile away at Sunnyside, the residence of Will Scott's aunt. It was while Wood was walking to school in the fall of 1866 that Samuel Zenas Ammen actually first met him. Ammen overheard Wood repeating a Latin phrase (which was the motto of Wood's first ritual) and translated it for him. It was this phrase that Ammen later drew inspiration from to develop the great theme of Kappa Alpha Order. In an 1866 essay that Wood read to Alpha Chapter, he gives insight into his thoughts on the purpose of his young K.A. Fraternity: "Let us be just, charitable and good. Let us be great by the prayers of widows and orphans rather than by their tears and lamentations. Let us be of one mind and faith, let us banish all that is evil and cling to all that is good. Let us pull together and pull hard, but above all things let there be no doubt that we are pulling right."

Because of the manner of his upbringing, Wood had a preference for activity and doing things that he enjoyed, at his own pace. Wood was not used to organized study. Ammen perceived Wood as "seeing the allegorical; the deep meaning;

and, the symbolism" of things. Unfortunately, Wood did not take to the environment of a formal education that Robert E. Lee was shaping as the new president of Washington College. In January of 1867, Lee contacted Wood's father and advised him that his son was not benefiting from the academic environment. Accordingly, Wood was called home by his father and resigned his chapter office as Number III on January 25, 1867. On February 1, Wood called his brothers together at the main building of Washington College and made a departing speech and a small presentation to the fraternity that he helped create. Wood remained at home at Woodlawn until 1871, becoming a Master Mason in his local lodge in 1869. He then began travels in the West and migrated to Missouri where he took part in the Grange Movement. In 1875, he returned to Woodlawn where he raised blooded stock. He married at the age of 40 and eventually had eight children. In addition to being a farmer and rancher, Wood became a justice of the peace, school board president, county judge, surveyor, and notary public and representative in the West Virginia State Assembly. He died on January 7, 1926, and is buried in the Ivanhoe Presbyterian Church Cemetery in Lost River, West Virginia.

__William Nelson Scott__ was born in Houston, Virginia, on September 25, 1848. He was the only other founder who was engaged in military service during the Civil War. Although his service, like Wood's, was limited, at the age of fifteen he became part of the reserves in Virginia. Will Scott was introduced to Wood by Rev. Scott, and the two young men became fast friends. He joined in Wood's evolving effort during the fall of 1865 to form a new society on campus. When the group formally organized, Will Scott, because of his impressive personality, was personally selected by Wood to be the fraternity's first president. He worked with Wood to guide the fledgling "lodge" through its trying first year. While it was Wood who first met S. Z. Ammen, it was Will Scott who convinced him to join the group of seven in October of 1866. Ammen said of Scott, "I have never seen any in equal to him in charm of voice, in solemnity of manner, in dignity of demeanor, or in general impressiveness in the initiatory customs." Will Scott presided over Ammen's initiation. After departing Washington Col-

lege, Scott entered Union Theological Seminary, where he completed his study and became a Presbyterian minister in 1872. After heading a parish in Richmond, Virginia, for a few years, Scott moved to Galveston, Texas, where he led the First Presbyterian Church for 19 years. During that time, he also served as a member of the Board of Trustees at Austin College. After surviving the Great Hurricane and Flood of 1900 that decimated the island and killed thousands, he returned to Staunton, Virginia, where he served as pastor of the Second Presbyterian Church until his death on June 3, 1919. Like Wood and the other founders, he also became a Freemason. He is buried in Hollywood Cemetery in Richmond, Virginia.

William Archibald Walsh *was born in Richmond, Virginia, on September 11, 1849. Although Walsh was not present when Will Scott first joined in Wood's idea of forming a new society, he soon was made aware of the idea and joined the effort. It was in Walsh's dorm room that Wood and Scott spent time between classes. The friendship that was cemented focused the group. On December 21, 1865, Wood proposed a toast to the "two Williams" upon which they "swore together" to form a society. Wood wrote, "The principal work of the first year was done in Walsh's room. Walsh was bright and capable, and he helped me a great deal, especially in connection with the badge." Because Walsh's family had resources, it is likely that he financed the first seven badges from Lexington jeweler D.M. Riley. Wood also spoke of the "many conferences in October and November while preliminary plans were laid." While he also revealed that "Christmas caused delay," it is important to note that the first meetings occurred in Walsh's quarters. After one year at Washington College, Walsh left in June of 1866 to take up his family's business as a merchant. The first document revealing the name of the group as "K.A." was issued to Walsh as a fees receipt in April of 1866. Walsh continued to correspond with Alpha Chapter, even after his departure, and is generally considered to be our first alumnus member. In 1874, Walsh became a Master Mason in Temple Lodge No. 9. Later that year, he traveled in Africa and returned home to Richmond in impaired health. He died in 1876 and also is buried in the Hollywood Cemetery.*

The Founding of Kappa Alpha Order - 1865

Stanhope McClelland Scott, the younger brother of Will, was not enrolled in school during the fall of 1865. However, he was "soon enlisted as he would enter Washington College in January." He was 15 years old at the time of our founding, making him the youngest founder. This occurrence set the minimum age for eligibility for membership in KA, which endures to this day. Stanhope graduated from Washington and Lee in 1871 and went on to study medicine at the University of Virginia. After receiving his medical license, he returned to his hometown to practice. Dr. Scott practiced medicine in western Maryland and northern West Virginia for over 50 years. He was the last of the four original founders to survive. He passed away on September 4, 1933, and is buried at Terra Alta, West Virginia. A leading member of the community, Stanhope was made a Mason in 1871, helped organize a lodge in Terra Alta and was elected its first Master.

The Beginning

The story of how Kappa Alpha Order began revolves around James Ward Wood's life experiences and influences. Wood planted the seed that Ammen culti-vated into our Order.

While Wood was born and raised in what is now West Virginia, his family aligned with the sentiments of Virginia, as Hardy County was actually only fifteen miles or so from the newly created state line. Since young Ward Wood was familiar with the countryside, he was assigned to patrol the borderland and to scout for the westward advance of the Federal Army. Ammen related that Wood's "service was limited, but useful." He believed that the military experience "made [Wood] confident." While at home on leave near the end of the war, Wood decided to ride out and visit a local girl. He prudently stuck his cavalry pistol into his boot as he was aware of dangers on mountain roads during wartime. As he mounted his horse, the pistol inadvertently discharged, wounding Wood's foot. Tragic as this event was, it was actually a blessing in disguise for Kappa Alpha Order. The wound was so severe that it ended Wood's military service.

19

Knights of the Order

As he recuperated during the spring and summer of 1865, Wood spent his time at the Lost River General Store. This country store, which still stands today, was a community center and a county office. There was a man at the store who was an incumbent in an important local office in Hardy County — he was apparently a great storyteller. He was also a Mason and a member of the Odd Fellows and a half dozen other secret societies. He fascinated young Wood with his stories of the lodge room. Ammen was convinced that "…every proceeding of these secret societies were unfolded" to Wood without scruple, so that the summer's recitals were equivalent to a course of lectures on the esoteric." Wood was captivated by secret societies and searched for more information about these brotherhoods. He had to look no further than his own father's library, and the Masonic book given to him by his Uncle Frank in 1861. In it, he found materials that likely fueled the fire of fraternalism within him.

On October 10, 1865, Wood arrived in Lexington and took up his residence on campus. Once enrolled in school, he soon discovered that two fraternities, Phi Kappa Psi and Beta Theta Pi, had reopened their chapters at Washington College. Ammen relates that Wood, drawing on his recent summer education, may have attempted to "petition" Phi Kappa Psi, as is the custom in Freemasonry. This may have caused him to be "criticized and even rejected by the aloof fraternity." Whatever occurred, Wood decided to form his own group. Since he was unfamiliar with fraternal organizations at the college level, Wood had nothing to draw from as a model. It is apparent that Wood was given the ritual of Epsilon Alpha, a small fraternity, founded at the University of Virginia in 1855, which had perished during the recent war. It had chapters "in at least five prominent Southern schools before the War" including Washington College. It is unknown when, or from whom, Wood received the "papers" of this fraternity; however, it is apparent that he reviewed their content and was struck by a core theme which mirrored his own life experience. From this concept, and rudimentary familiarity with ritualistic intent, Wood constructed a brief ceremony that was soon put to use. It is uncertain as to the exact date that Wood completed the first ritual. He later wrote that, "there were many conferences in October and November while

preliminary plans were made." However, it is well-established that on December 21, 1865, three of our founders met and formally bound their friendship by a "mutual pledge of faith and loyalty" as Wood made his "toast to the two Williams" standing before a warm fireplace in William Walsh's small room at the "southernmost end" of the "Old South Dorm."

Wood chose the name for the new group and called it Phi Kappa Chi. The name had no meaning and it is likely that Wood merely chose it to rival the popular Phi Kappa Psi, whose members had been rude to him. Though Will Scott may have assisted somewhat, the ritual of the first fraternity was primarily drafted by Wood. The ceremony he penned was brief but contained a great theme which endures even today. The ritual never mentioned the name Phi Kappa Chi, nor made any allusion to it. In fact, the ceremony communicated a life philosophy more than identity with a name. Wood organized the group and selected his friend Will Scott as the first Number I; Walsh, Number II; and Wood, Number III. Wood reported that "Christmas delayed the group somewhat," but they became known as a fraternity in the spring of 1866. The other societies at Washington College resented the appearance of a new secret society on campus. Phi Kappa Psi was especially perturbed at Wood's choice of a name for the group. Wood soon realized that his brotherhood was growing and needed a separate identity. By April of 1866, Wood chose the letters "K.A." for his "Lodge." Like Phi Kappa Chi, "K.A." initially had no meaning but the obvious one. Private letters written by early members of Alpha Chapter indicate that Wood likely selected K.A. for its immediate recognition. The popular old antebellum society, Kuklos Adelphon, founded at the University of North Carolina in 1812, had all but perished during the recent war, but its reputation was well known in the South. Kuklos Adelphon was more than a mere college fraternity. Its "Circles" met in communities long after its members left college campuses. Wood was aware of this and the concept of a lifelong "Circle of Brothers" had great appeal to him. The new organization began to grow and it had initiated seven additional members by the end of the 1866 spring term. The other fraternities were obviously intimidated by the presence of K.A. for in May of 1866, Wood was approached by a senior

professor at the college, a member of Phi Kappa Psi, who urged him to abandon his efforts. Wood respectfully declined that offer.

Transformation

The 1866-67 school year brought promise to Washington College and KA Largely because of Lee's presidency at the school, the enrollment more than doubled to nearly 400 students. KA initiated seven more members into its group that fall. On the evening of October 17, 1866, twenty-two year-old Samuel Zenas Ammen of Fincastle, Virginia became a member of KA. Ammen was no ordinary student; because of his intellect, he was given advance standing when he arrived at Washington College, and he was a veteran of the Army of Northern Virginia and its Navy, as well. Ammen was a serious student, immaculate in appearance and precise in manner. He was very confident, and Will Scott, who bestowed nicknames on his brothers, dubbed him "Lord." Ammen's initiation into this early group was conducted with a revised version of the ritual first penned by Wood. It is clear from his own writings that while Ammen was certainly moved by certain parts of the ceremony, he felt that it was too brief and uninspiring. Ammen had significant fraternal experience. He had been made a Master Mason in his hometown lodge in Fincastle in 1865. As a Mason, he was well versed in organized ritual which had been refined over hundreds of years. Ammen would later say that this first ritual had "nothing to touch the imagination of initiates nor stir their fancy." However, Ammen was inspired by the possibilities of this young fraternity and its members whom he greatly respected. He urged the society to enhance its initiation ceremonies and was soon selected by his chapter brothers to take an active role in those efforts.

In Wood's room at Sunnyside in November 1866, Ammen and Wood discussed possibilities for a new ritual, and it was agreed that Ammen should continue the work. At Ammen's suggestion, the chapter approved a new meaning for KA on November 23, 1866. The chapter placed its confidence in Ammen and he, along with Wood and Will Scott, was appointed to a committee to review the ritual in its entirety. In order to gather material, Ammen received Wood's ritual,

observed the chapter's activities and listened to their collective ideals and beliefs. He was particularly impressed by an essay presented to the chapter by Wood on November 30, 1866, wherein the life of the ancient Order of Knights Templar was detailed as a model of inspiration for the group's purpose. Ammen, Scott, and Wood conferred on several occasions, many times late into the night. Wood presented Ammen with the "papers" that he had written and Ammen preserved a few of its impressive parts and began construction of a new ritual, with a new vehicle for communicating the great theme of KA.

Nearly two decades later, Will Scott would write to Ammen, "The Ritual was all so altered, changed and improved upon, mainly by you, that we can say it underwent a complete regeneration, or new birth." Ammen later related that Wood was completely deferential to his advanced experience with the esoteric. Indeed, Wood's departure from school was only a few weeks away. Wood's own correspondence with the Order over the remainder of his life indicates that he confidently left the fraternity he began under the stewardship of Ammen.

Wood never hesitated to credit Ammen with transforming his K.A. «Lodge» into the Order of national prominence that it remains today. Ammen's constant refinement of the ritual and creation of the constitution, by-laws, grip, symbols and regalia of the Order, along with his lifelong commitment ultimately earned him the title of Practical Founder of Kappa Alpha Order. Ammen later revealed, "Material for my work was gathered from many sources – books, chapter experience and essays read at chapter meetings. During this formative period, the ruling ideas were suggested mainly by the ideas and aspirations expressed in essays of leading members. The present ritual, in fact, was not made; it grew." It grew from a seed planted by Wood. The new ritual transformed K.A. into Kappa Alpha Order, an order of Christian knights (first inspired by Wood's November 1866 essay to Alpha Chapter and set to work by Ammen) pledged to the highest ideals of character and personal achievement. Ammen and his Alpha Chapter brothers sought to preserve the virtues of chivalry, respect for others, honor, duty, integrity and reverence for God and woman.

Despite the milestone of establishing a solid identity and presence at

Washington College, the young Order was not without the startup problems typical with most new organizations. Indeed, the brothers of Old Alpha stood at a crossroads. The chapter expelled members who violated their obligations and were not strong enough to endure growing pains. Will Scott, the chapter's first Number I, was preparing to leave Lexington to attend seminary, and the chapter brothers had to decide whether they should keep up the effort.

One moonlit night in May 1867, Ammen and Jo Lane Stern, a recent initiate with whom he had become fast friends, were taking one of many walks they enjoyed together throughout their lives. This particular evening, they were discussing the future of their young fraternity. They paused along the way, and sat on the steps of White's General Store, on the corner of Lexington's Main and Nelson streets. There, they seriously contemplated the viability of Kappa Alpha and whether or not they should continue the chapter. They asked, "Shall we let the Lodge die?" Ammen well-remembered that conversation and later recalled, "The outcome was a decision to keep up the fight, and from that time on our prospects improved." Clearly, Ammen and Stern spearheaded that effort. For that reason, Stern is appropriately given a status on par with our founders.

With the fortitude to forge ahead, the chapter began the 1867-1868 school year with Ammen as the new Number I. They began looking beyond Washington College to establish KA's second chapter; their first prospect was naturally the school's neighbor, the Virginia Military Institute. An invitation for membership was extended to John E. Hollingsworth, a VMI cadet, and by spring 1868, three more cadets were initiated. Subsequently, Beta Chapter was formed March 8, 1868.

Transfers from Washington College established chapters at the University of Georgia (Gamma) in 1868 and at Wofford College (Delta) in Spartanburg, South Carolina, in 1869. Epsilon also was established in 1869 at Emory University in Atlanta by members of Gamma. Stern recalled that that Lee permitted him to miss class and travel to Ashland, Virginia, in 1869 to found Zeta at Randolph-Macon College. Although Lee was known for only permitting absences because of illness, it is believed that he approved Stern's journey to Randolph-

The Founding of Kappa Alpha Order - 1865

Macon and then again to Richmond College in 1870.

Stern stated that he arrived in Richmond amid little enthusiasm for fraternities, but that he brought with him a letter of introduction from Lee to J.L.M. Curry, an influential law professor, which explained his mission. Allegedly, Curry called a faculty meeting and announced, "If General Lee will let a man come away to establish a chapter, I vote for it. If he thinks a fraternity is a good thing, I think so, too." Thus, Eta was born. Theta (prime) was also established in 1870 at Atlanta's Oglethorpe University by members of Gamma and Epsilon chapters. By the close of 1870, five years after KA's founding, the Order's ranks had grown to eight chapters.

In 1870, Ammen's efforts finally achieved the permanence of ink in Kappa Alpha's first publication. A copy of the forty-six page booklet, which contained the Order's constitution, ritual and bylaws, was sent to each chapter. Called the "Green Book" because of its green paper cover, the publication established the "General Council," now called Convention. The first Convention was held that same year in Richmond, Virginia, where Ammen presided in a dual capacity as Number I of Alpha Chapter and as Knight Commander (our national president).

By 1870, Kappa Alpha Order had in place the essential organizational procedures that endure to this day. It had survived various crisis's and was on the way to growing into the organization that exists today.

Knights of the Order

IV.
The Citadel Reborn: 1865-1882

*I*n the years after the War, various attempts were made to re-open The Citadel, all to no avail. The Citadel was occupied by Federal troops, money was scarce and with a Reconstruction government in place, no action was taken. Thus, from 1865-1877, when Reconstruction ended, the academy remained dormant.

In April, 1877, a small group of graduates living near Charleston met to explore the re-opening of The Citadel. Further meetings followed and the group expanded its membership. An Association of Graduates was organized with Brigadier General Johnson Hagood '47 as President. It was this group, led by General Hagood, who finally succeeded in getting the school re-opened in 1882.

 One of the most treasured relics of Citadel history was a flag given to the Corps of Cadets by the Washington Light Infantry. The two military brotherhoods had a close affinity with each other. On February 22, 1857, the 50th anniversary of the founding of the Washington Light Infantry, they presented a specially made flag to the Corps. It was made of blue Lyons silk with the arms of the State of South Carolina and the name, "South Carolina Military Academy" on the front side. On the reverse side was a wreath of oak leaves with the inscription, "Fort Moultrie, King's Mountain, Eutaw Springs" and below that the words, "Our Heritage."

From 1857 to 1865, this flag was in use by the Corps in both peace and war. It was sent to Columbia for safekeeping late in the war where it narrowly escaped being burned by Sherman's troops. It was in possession of the retreating battalion of cadets in February, 1865 as they moved north from the capitol. As the war came to a close, it was finally placed with Captain John Peyre Thomas for safekeeping.

Some years later, Captain Thomas opened the Carolina Military Institute in Charlotte, North Carolina and the flag was used by that school for a few years. Captain Thomas ultimately delivered the flag in 1882 to the re-opened Citadel of which he was the new Superintendent. The Battalion flag entrusted to Captain, (now Colonel) John Peyre Thomas after the War, may still be seen in The Citadel Museum today.

Governor Wade Hampton actively supported efforts to re-open the school by appointing a new Board of Visitors on April 18, 1878. General Johnson Hagood was appointed chairman and he spearheaded efforts to get approval from the federal government for return of the Citadel property. By early 1882, this had been accomplished and efforts to build a faculty and staff for the school were begun. By August, the Board of Visitors announced the school would reopen in

October and on September 1, 1882, when Colonel Thomas officially assumed the post of Superintendent the Battalion flag was hanging in his office.[1]

On October 2, 1882, 189 cadets reported for duty at The Citadel. Of those, 104 were pay cadets, 66 were beneficiary cadets and there were 19 others appointed by the Board of Visitors.[2] The enlightened beneficiary cadet program was retained and slightly modified with the reopening. The *quid pro quo* for beneficiary cadets was no longer the duty to guard the states military supplies. Instead, new beneficiary cadets were obligated to teach in a free public school for two years after graduation.[3]

The years from 1882-1892 were important ones for The Citadel. Life returned to normal with academic and facilities improvements being stressed. During that 10 year period, a total of 655 cadets were enrolled. Of those, 423 were pay and 232 were beneficiary. 298 pay cadets and 56 beneficiary cadets withdrew prior to graduation. Nine cadets died in school. 53 pay cadets and 104 beneficiary cadets graduated. There were a total of 69 pay cadets and 66 beneficiary cadets enrolled on December 20, 1892.[4]

The Citadel had been blessed during its earlier existence with great men overseeing its growth and direction. Such was the case when it reopened in 1882. General Johnson Hagood had served with great distinction in the War and subsequently served two terms as Comptroller General of the state. Following that he was elected Governor, serving until 1882. General Johnson Hagood then served as Chairman of the Board of Visitors from the re-opening of the school in 1882 until his death in 1898.

Knights of the Order

Endnotes

1. Thomas p.344

2. Thomas, p. 349

3. Thomas, p. 339

4. Thomas, p 522

V.
Robert E. Lee, Kappa Alpha Order and The Citadel

*J*t is entirely fitting that Kappa Alpha Order established a chapter at the Citadel in 1883. After all, these two unique organizations shared values that had much in common. Among those values were:

- Excellence in all things and a constant striving to improve oneself.

- An acknowledgment that man is subservient to a Supreme Being.

- Patriotism or service to one's country is an obligation of citizenship.

- Respect for others, especially women and children.

General Robert E. Lee

- Honor, that word for doing the right thing, even when it is not popular or convenient.

- Humility, demonstrating a quiet strength of character with a humble demeanor.

It is also fitting that Robert E. Lee is looked upon as the "Spiritual Founder" of Kappa Alpha Order. After all, General Lee epitomizes the values set forth above and his life was one dedicated to living those values. Winston Churchill called Lee, "the noblest American who ever lived."

He demonstrated **Honor** and **Patriotism** when, in the spring of 1861, he declined the command of all the Union Armies in order to support his native State. Lee must have known the risks the South faced in a war with the overwhelming population and military resources of the North. He must have known that strategically the South was outmatched and would likely lose the conflict. He would also have imagined the accolades and tributes he would have received as the Union commander. Yet, he could not draw his sword against his neighbors and kin and chose the difficult path of supporting his state.

He demonstrated **Respect** for others when he issued orders to the Army of Northern Virginia prior to invading Pennsylvania in the summer of 1863. Everywhere Union armies had penetrated the South, they had waged war on defenseless civilians. Burning and pillaging civilian homes and businesses, the Union conducted war without mercy or boundaries. Lee would have none of it. Despite a clamor of southern voices for retribution, he would not allow the Army of Northern Virginia to wage war in that manner. On June 27, 1863, he issued General Order No. 7, forbidding his soldiers from waging war on the *"innocent and defenseless"*. As he put it, *"It must be remembered that we make war only upon armed men, and that we cannot take vengeance for the wrongs our people have suffered without lowering ourselves in the eyes of all whose abhorrence has been excited by the atrocities of our enemy and offending against Him to whom vengeance belongeth, and without whose favor and support our efforts must all prove in vain"*.

Lee demonstrated **Humility** both in the manner of the surrender at Appomattox and his choice of the Presidency of Washington College. At Appomattox, Lee was the vanquished general, but his calm presence and courageous decisions made the officers of Grant's staff look on him with awe.

Robert E. Lee, Kappa Alpha Order and The Citadel

His General Order No.9, dated April 10, 1865 to the Army of Northern Virginia, is a repudiation of more futile bloodletting and a farewell to his beloved Army.

"After four years of arduous service, marked by unsurpassed courage and fortitude, the Army of Northern Virginia has been compelled to yield to overwhelming numbers and resources. I need not tell the survivors of so many hard fought battles, who have remained steadfast to the last, that I have consented to this result from no distrust of them; but feeling that valour and devotion could accomplish nothing that could compensate for the loss that would have attended the continuation of the contest, I have determined to avoid the useless sacrifice of those whose past services have endeared them to their countrymen. By the terms of the agreement, officers and men can return to their homes and remain there until exchanged. You will take with you the satisfaction that proceeds from the consciousness of duty faithfully performed; and I earnestly pray that a merciful God will extend to you His blessing and protection. With an increasing admiration of your constancy and devotion to your country, and a grateful remembrance of your kind and generous consideration of myself, I bid you an affectionate farewell."

While other prominent war leaders wrote books and entered the business world to make money, Lee took the humble job of helping to educate a new generation of young men of the South.

Lee epitomized the term **"Excelsior"** meaning a constant striving for improvement and higher values- a motto of Kappa Alpha Order. When asked by a new student what the rules were at Washington College, Lee replied, "We have but one rule here, and it is that every student must be a gentleman."

Robert E. Lee, throughout his life acknowledged God. He often made reference to prayer in challenging circumstances and made reference to a "merciful God" in his farewell message to the Army.

Knights of the Order

Finally, on a rainy night in late September, 1870 he was taken ill. As Senior Warden, he had just attended a vestry meeting at Grace Church in Lexington. He died on October 12, 1870 and he and his family are now buried in the crypt of Lee Chapel on the Washington & Lee University campus.

In 1907, on the centennial of Lee's birth, Dr. Edward S. Joynes, in an address at the University of South Carolina, asked this question:

"Would you follow Lee? No more, on the embattled field, can he lead you, as he led your fathers to glorious victory; but in spirit and in eternal fame he still lives – the Christian soldier, the self-sacrificing patriot, the college president, the South's noblest gentleman – to remind you, by example as by precept, that "Duty is the sublimest word in the language."

"To think of Robert E. Lee allows us to hope for more out of ourselves and our children. The bright star of Lee still lifts our gaze. His example of a life led by honor, devotion to duty, and gentlemanly conduct is, and should be, an inspiration to us all."

Robert E. Lee was the living example of the True Gentleman and Christian Knight.

VI.
History of the Theta
Chapter Charter

*A*s the Kappa Alpha Order grew from the original Alpha (1st) chapter at Washington College, (now Washington & Lee University) in 1865, it expanded to new chapters using the Greek alphabet as a numbering system. Thus, Beta (2nd) chapter was established at Virginia Military Institute in 1868, Gamma (3rd) chapter was established at the University of Georgia in 1868, Delta (4th) chapter was established at Wofford College in 1869, Epsilon (5th) chapter was established at Emory University in 1869, Zeta (6th) chapter was established at Randolph Macon College in 1869 and Zeta (7th) chapter was established at Richmond College in 1870.

On December, 25, 1870, the eighth chapter of the Kappa Alpha Order, Theta, was authorized at Oglethorpe University in Atlanta, Georgia. This charter was signed by the Knight Commander at the time, Samuel Z. Ammen, who became known as the Practical Founder of the Order. Records indicate that ten men were initiated into Theta before the school closed and the chapter folded in December, 1872.

Over the following years, other chapters were formed and the Greek numbering system was continued using Iota (9th), Kappa (10th), Lambda (11th) and others. The name, Theta, became dormant.

As previously noted, The Citadel was re-opened in October, 1882. It appears that efforts to establish a Kappa Alpha chapter at the school began as soon as it re-opened. Credit for this effort goes to Philip Bascom Hamer, a graduate of Wofford College. Brother Hamer was born on December 13, 1860 in Marborough (now Marlboro) County, S.C. He was educated in Bennettsville, S.C. and entered the freshman class at Wofford in 1878, graduating in 1882. From July, 1882 to June,

1883, Philip Hamer taught at two different local grammar schools. Following his brief teaching career, he began the study of law and was admitted to the South Carolina Bar in late 1884. During the remainder of his legal career, Mr. Hamer practiced law in Bennettsville and Marion, S.C. In addition to his law practice, he also edited and owned the Pee Dee Index, a popular newspaper in the area.

His involvement with Kappa Alpha Order began during his freshman year in college when he was initiated into Delta chapter at Wofford College. In 1880, he helped establish Sigma chapter (Davidson College). He held several offices in his chapter in college and attended the Kappa Alpha Conventions of 1881 and 1883. From 1883-1885, he edited *The Magazine of Kappa Alpha*. Philip Hamer later served as Knight Commander of the Order from 1887 to 1889.

Sometime in 1882-1883, Philip Hamer applied to the Governor of South Carolina for formal permission to establish a Kappa Alpha chapter at the newly re-opened Citadel. His request was turned down because of existing regulations prohibiting secret societies among the cadets. That did not deter Hamer, as it was decided to establish a chapter *sub rosa*, and he then recruited the cadets who would become the original charter members. Those men were William Edward Dick, Francis Ovid Spain, and Paul Hout Tamplet, all of whom had entered school in October, 1882.

What influence Philip Hamer had on the selection of a chapter name is unknown. At any rate, the name of Theta was available since Oglethorpe University had gone out of business in 1872. A charter was issued to the men assembled at The Citadel naming it Theta chapter. The charter was dated October 1, 1883, which coincided with the beginning of the second year of classes at The Citadel. This charter was the 23rd charter to be issued by the young Kappa Alpha Order. (Delta Chapter at Wofford College is credited through Philip

Hamer with being the sponsor of Theta chapter at The Citadel.)

As we now know, the Theta chapter at The Citadel was closed in 1890. In a twist of fate, Oglethorpe University later re-opened and another Kappa Alpha chapter was established there in 1918. It was not renamed Theta, but instead, was called Beta Nu. This became the 67th charter to be issued by Kappa Alpha.

Finally, in 1893, just three years after The Citadel's Theta charter was surrendered, a chapter was formed at the University of Kentucky and it was given the designation of Theta. This was the 40th chapter of Kappa Alpha Order formed.

To avoid confusion in the use by these several institutions of the name "Theta", the common reference to each is as follows. It should be pointed out that at the time, the terms "Prime" and "Second" were not used.

Theta Prime- Oglethorpe University - 1870-1872.

Theta Second- The Citadel - 1883-1890.

Theta Chapter- University of Kentucky - 1893 to present.

Theta Commission- The Citadel - 2008 to present.

Knights of the Order

VII.
The Theta Second Charter

*A*s with the beginning and the early years of any new organization, documentation and formalization can be haphazard. So it was with the preparation of the document called a charter by the early leaders of Kappa Alpha Order. For the first several years of Kappa Alpha's existence, the individual chapters were not even given a written charter. Gamma chapter at The University of Georgia was the first to be given a written charter in 1868. From 1868 until 1894, all charters were hand written. After 1894, each chapter was presented with an engraved, attractive charter. Below is the expected text for a typical hand written charter in the 1880 time period that would be similar to that issued to Theta Second chapter at The Citadel in 1883.

Charter

To all whom it may concern, be it known by these presents that:

I hereby charter, sanction and recognize the Lodge of Knights at The Citadel as legally established under the name and title of Theta Lodge of Kappa Alpha Order and

That the brethren to whom this charter is granted do pledge themselves and their successors to observe and preserve unaltered the Initiation Rites and Constitution received from the Knight Commander, to recognize and fraternize with no society or pretended Lodge not working under a charter granted by the Knight Commander of this Order

To maintain peace and unity with all Lodges of this Order; to recognize the authority of its General Officers and return this charter to the Knight Commandeer when demanded by him according to law.

Knights of the Order

Granted this 1ˢᵗ day of October, 1883 to the Worthy Knights

William Edward Dick

Francis Ovid Spain

Paul Hout Tamplet

By: J.S. Candler, Knight Commander of the Kappa Alpha Order

VIII.
Customs and Practices

*T*he first officers in Alpha Chapter used Roman Numerals to designate their positions in the earliest minutes on record. That system perpetuated itself until today. For instance, the Kappa Alpha designation for President is simply Number I. (pronounced "One"). The positions are designated in this manner for active chapters. The broader Theta Commission of later years adopted this same nomenclature for its various officers. Since these designations are used extensively in this book, it may be helpful to the reader to outline those offices and their designations.

Number I. President

Number II. Vice-President

Number III. Recording Secretary

Number IV. Corresponding Secretary

Number V. Historian

Number VI. Purser

Number VII. Parliamentarian

Number VIII. Sergeant at Arms

Number IX. Marshal

Number X. Musician (unique to Theta Commission)

Number XI. Chaplain (unique to Theta Commission)

During the early years of Kappa Alpha, record keeping and office

details were understandably lacking. This is particularly true of the 1883-1890 initiates. It was only later that each initiate was assigned a permanent badge number and the specific date of their initiation was recorded. Thus, the 1920-1924 and later initiates have badge numbers and specific initiation dates, while the earlier initiates do not.

School years back then did not begin in August or September, but near the first of October. Midterm examinations were in February rather than December. The end of the school year was in July rather than early May as it typically is now.

As the number of Kappa Alpha chapters increased in each state and men began to graduate, the need of some type of alumni organization became evident. Local alumni organizations were established in many of the cities and towns in which active Chapters existed. For instance, there would be a Kappa Alpha alumni organization in Columbia, S.C. where Rho chapter operated at the University of South Carolina. Initially, these local alumni organizations were not formally controlled by the Kappa Alpha hierarchy. Once a state had several of these alumni organizations in existence there developed a need to coordinate their efforts. Thus, was born a Kappa Alpha State Association of South Carolina. (*Journal V,* p.117.)

The *Journal* reports that "Pursuant to a call sent out to the different chapters and alumni members in this state, a number of staunch Kappa Alpha's met in Columbia, S.C. on the 12th of November, 1884 and formed an organization under the style and title of "the Kappa Alpha State Association of South Carolina." They elected a full slate of officers and adopted a constitution. The object of the organization was to "have a reunion of the members at least once a year. All persons who have been initiated into the Order and who reside in South Carolina are eligible for membership."

Customs and Practices

The Kappa Alpha Order coat of arms, officially adopted in 1897, bears the phrase "Dieu et les Dames" which translates to "God and the Ladies". This reflects the reverence a knight should have for his maker and all women. The Order's official flowers are the red rose and the white magnolia. Within Kappa Alpha circles a tradition has grown to refer to one's loved one as their "Kappa Alpha Rose." Therefore, a brother's wife or girlfriend is referred to as his Kappa Alpha Rose.

Knights of the Order

IX.
The Kappa Alpha Journal

*T*he Convention of 1878 decided to create a magazine/newsletter to facilitate communication between the fraternity, its various chapters and individual members. Thus, was born in 1879, The *Kappa Alpha Journal*. After publishing three magazines in 1879, the operation folded and was not resumed until 1883. At that time, it was called the *Magazine of Kappa Alpha*. In 1885, it changed its name back to The *Kappa Alpha Journal* and has used that name ever since.

Publication times varied over the years, sometimes it was a bi-monthly, other times it was published every month during the school year.

The format for the Journal has evolved over the years, but a key feature has always been the reports from the individual chapters. Each chapter had an officer known as the IV (Four) or "Number Four," whose role was Corresponding Secretary. The "C.S.", as he was known, prepared and submitted each month, news from his chapter. Thus, in theory, each chapter knew of the activities of other chapters and bound the brothers of the scattered chapters together.

Theta Second had several Corresponding Secretaries over the years. Some were more diligent than others in sending in reports to the Journal.

Another category in each Journal was the "Personal" section to which a member could send short personal information of note for publication. This section recorded such things as jobs held, honors garnered, marriages, births and deaths.

Knights of the Order

X.
The Kappa Alpha Directory and Catalogue

*I*n the age before the internet and online information, the only way to learn the history of the Kappa Alpha Order and details of the membership of the Kappa Alpha chapters scattered across the country was through some written compilation of information. Thus, was born the ***Kappa Alpha Directory and Catalogue***. In 1870, the Knight Commander was given the duty to "compile and have printed statistics and catalogues showing the general condition of the Order." In 1874, the office of Grand Historian was created to collect and preserve the history of the Order. Subsequently, in 1885, each chapter was authorized to have its own historian.

The original plan was to prepare and print a catalogue annually. However, finances prevented the achievement of this goal. For the first 13 years of the existence of the Order, only three General Catalogues were published to outline the Order's history and membership. For the next 13 years from 1878-1891 no catalogues were published. Finally, in 1891, a General Catalogue was printed and made available to the membership. An Annual or General Catalogue has been printed on a more or less regular basis since then.

Most Catalogues contained a history of the fraternity's founding, its programs, Conventions, officers past and present and other useful information. The most valuable part of each catalogue was a listing of each chapter, its individual members and their current occupation and biographical information.

Knights of the Order

XI.
Secret Societies and
Anti-Fraternity Laws

lmost from the beginning of the South Carolina Military Academy its leaders have been wary of unauthorized social organizations in the Corps of Cadets. This concern became codified in 1849, when General James Jones was Chairman of the Board of Visitors and Major R. W. Colcock was Superintendent. Regulation 188 was promulgated to provide as follows:

"188. No society shall be organized among the Cadets, without special license from the Superintendent, nor shall any assembly of Cadets be held, for this or any other purpose, without his express permission promulgated in orders."

In 1859, this Regulation was re-numbered to No. 199, but the language remained the same.

When the Citadel re-opened in October, 1882, General Johnson Hagood was Chairman of the Board of Visitors and Colonel John P. Thomas was Superintendent. Regulation 192 was adopted stating:

Colonel Oliver James Bond, President

49

"Paragraph 192. Societies: No society shall be organized among the cadets without special license from the Superintendent; nor shall any assembly of Cadets be held, for this or any other purpose, without his express permission promulgated in orders. Any society organized by Cadets for literary purposes will receive the sanction of the Academy, but its rules and regulations must be in accordance with the Code of the Academy."

This same Regulation continued in effect in 1887 when Hagood was still Chairman, and General George D. Johnston was Superintendent.

Secret societies are defined as groups whose membership, rituals and inner workings are not available to the general public. Social fraternities became popular in institutions of higher education after the War Between The States. By their nature and due to the competitive aspect of their activities, most kept their activities secret. In fact, members usually had to sign or pledge an oath to safeguard the fraternities' secrets. Hence, these otherwise college social clubs became known as "secret societies."

There was opposition to these organizations by institutions of higher learning for several reasons. First, each student was obligated first to obey his or her college regulations. Fraternities with their secret rituals constituted a threat to the obedience to college regulations. Secondly, because membership in fraternities was selective there existed an unhealthy division and friction between fraternity and non-fraternity students.

If the issue of fraternities posed a problem for civilian colleges, they were anathema to military colleges such as The Citadel and the Virginia Military Institute. Military organizations operated by a strict chain of command. In a military unit, there was one set of rules and loyalties that applied to everyone equally and extended to everyone

in that structure. Having a group of individuals inside the organization with separate, deep, loyalties to another organization was heresy. Further, having several separate fraternities competing for members within the organization while including some and not others led to friction and poor morale.

College Regulations in effect at The Citadel upon its re-opening in 1882 reflect these concerns.

As young men are want to do, Cadets of that day interpreted paragraph 192 to mean that they were not expressly prohibited from joining a "society", but merely that if caught they might expect punishment for doing so, as with any other minor violation .

As noted in some of the Theta chapter reports to The Kappa Alpha Journal, non-fraternity men were called "barbarians", often shorted to "barbs." This derision undoubtedly contributed to friction on campus between the minority of Cadets who were in fraternities and the majority of cadets who were not.

Citadel President (1908-1930) Colonel Oliver J. Bond captures the military's concerns about fraternities on pages 112 -113 of his book, *The Story of The Citadel*, published in 1932. He writes,

"There was one feature of college student life which was very popular in the civil institutions of learning, but which was not adapted to a military regime. A number of sub-rosa chapters of Greek letter fraternities were organized at The Citadel in the 80's, but it was early perceived that their influence was not beneficent. In a small student body, where every individual was well known to every other, and where the relations of the cadets were those of a common family life, any separation into different social groups led inevitably to rivalries and antagonisms, which reacted unfavorably on discipline and the morale of the Corps. The immortal words attributed to Lee, DUTY IS THE SUBLIMEST WORD

IN THE ENGLISH LANGUAGE" were framed and hung on the guard-room wall where every cadet on duty must perforce read them; and undoubtedly it inspired many a cadet officer to perform his military functions with strictness and impartiality. But there were others not so strong, and when an officer of the day was conveniently unobservant of the delinquencies of a fellow fraternity man, while zealous enough to report others, his integrity as an officer was properly questioned by the corps."

Bond continued, *"In time, too, there arose a serious division of the cadets into Frats and Non-frats, with intimations of social distinctions which had no place in a democratic body where character, ability and industry were the only criteria of merit."*

He then concluded, *"The Board of Visitors wisely took measures to abolish and ban the fraternities, an action later approved by the legislature, which enacted a law prohibiting them in all State institutions of learning. This law lately has been repealed, but opinion at The Citadel has not changed."*

While the above comments of Colonel Bond were written in 1930, when he was a retired former President, his views of fraternities were different in 1886, when as a cadet, he was initiated into the *sub rosa* Sigma Alpha Epsilon chapter at The Citadel.[1] No mention is made in his book of his own fraternity experiences as a cadet. Nevertheless, Colonel Bond's observations are correct as concern the incompatibility of fraternities with the military environment.

With faculty support and approval, in the 1860s, 1870s and 1880s many colleges passed regulations prohibiting fraternities. (Citadel Regulations; Paragraph 192). This was followed by some states, including South Carolina, outlawing fraternities and secret societies by state statute. By Act No. 322, passed by the General Assembly of South Carolina in 1897, and strongly supported by Governor "Pitch-fork Ben" Tillman, such societies were banned.

Secret Societies and Anti-Fraternity Laws

The Act said, "...the Governing Boards of all institutions of higher learning in South Carolina, supported in whole or in part by public funds be, and are hereby are required to forbid and disallow in their respective institutions such secret Greek letter fraternities or all organizations of a similar nature: Provided, nothing herein contained shall interfere with the literary societies in such institutions." This Act was approved the 5th day of March, 1897.

The mechanism for the enforcement of these laws is found in the matriculation pledge to be signed by each student, which forbids a student, while a student, to become a member of a secret society or organization existing, in or outside the school. The student was also prohibited from attending any meetings of such societies or wearing badges of same. The Citadel had such a pledge as did the Virginia Military Institute.

Many of the fraternities, especially those in South Carolina, were forced to operate *sub rosa*, that is, undercover, in order to carry on. Such was the case of Theta Chapter at The Citadel during its entire existence. As an example of its *sub rosa* status, in each issue of The Kappa Alpha Journal of this period, there was published a listing of each Chapter Secretary. Consistently, during the 1880s under the Chapter Secretary listing for Theta Chapter there is a blank with the ominous notation, "Name and address can be had on application." Thus, the Corresponding Secretary of Theta chapter, while sending in a report of the activities of chapter members, kept his own name secret. The Beta chapter of Kappa Alpha Order at the Virginia Military Institute operated in the same manner.

It was not until April 4, 1927, that the General Assembly by Act No. 126 rescinded Act 322 and the legal prohibition against fraternities was reversed. Nevertheless, for valid reasons, The Citadel maintains to this day a ban on social fraternities among cadets on campus through its own regulations.

Knights of the Order

(Authors note: For an excellent discussion of general fraternity activity in the 1880's, the reader is referred to Major Steven Smith's article in *The Citadel Alumni News*, Spring, 2013.)

Endnotes

1. Smith, *Alumni News,* Spring-Summer, 2013, p. 21

XII.
Theta Second Chapter: 1883-1885

*H*aving obtained a charter for Theta chapter, Philip Hamer recruited three cadets as its charter members. On October 1, 1883, Theta initiated its first members. They were Cadets William Edward Dick, Francis Ovid Spain and Paul Hout Tamplet. According to Kappa Alpha lore, William Ernest Lucas assisted by George Alexander Norwood performed the initiation.[1]

William Ernest Lucas was a native of Darlington, S.C., located near the home of Philip Hamer and a member of Delta Chapter (initiated in 1881) at Wofford College. Since Delta was the "sponsor" of the new Theta chapter, under the guidance of Hamer, the selection of Lucas to perform the rites made sense. George Alexander Norwood, who assisted Lucas, was a native of Hartsville, S.C. and a member of Tau chapter (initiated in 1881) at Wake Forest University. Again, the choice of Norwood appears to be based on friendship and proximity as Norwood resided in Hartsville, not far from both Marion, (Hamer's hometown) and Darlington, (Lucas's hometown). Thus, by the beginning of the school year in 1883, Theta had its first members and became operational.

Between October, 1883 and the end of 1884, Theta prospered with the initiation of ten other cadets. They were, Armstrong Jolly Howard, William Jennings, Kenneth Gordon Matheson, all of whom were initiated by the end of 1883. In 1884, seven other cadets were brought into the Order. They were George Williams Allison, Council Black Ashley, Thomas Perrin Harrison, Francis Parker Huger, Evander McIvar Law, Benjamin Munnerlyn and Edward Frost Parker. These thirteen men of Theta were chosen from a student body consisting of only 175 cadets.

Theta was actually the second fraternity chartered at The Citadel. The Alpha Chi chapter of Alpha Tau Omega was the first, being chartered on January 1, 1883. Finally, on December 13, 1883, the Lambda chapter of Sigma Alpha Epsilon was chartered. These were later joined by Theta chapter of Sigma Nu in 1886 and the Lambda chapter of Pi Kappa Alpha in 1889.[2]

The History and Catalogue of 1891 quotes a letter written by Francis Ovid Spain that possibly explains the atmosphere in which the chapter operated. *"We were so circumstanced that few meetings were held and few records kept during our brief existence. We were more like a large family of brothers, who dwelt together in love and unity of the closest kind, than a regular business organization."* Others had a more positive outlook. William Edward Dick referred to Theta as the *"Banner"* chapter, indicating it was strong.[3]

Nevertheless, in 1885 and 1886, there were no initiations performed by Theta Chapter. We now know that there were other fraternities operating *sub rosa* on the Citadel campus during this period, including ΣAE (Sigma Alpha Epsilon) and ATΩ (Alpha Tau Omega).

The History and Catalogue of 1891 indicates that in late 1884, the Superintendent (now known as the President) of The Citadel became aware of the fraternities and *"the various chapters were forced to give up their charters."*

Colonel John Peyre Thomas
Courtesy: The Citadel Archives & Museum, Charleston, SC

Theta Second Chapter: 1883 - 1885

How the Superintendent (at the time, Colonel John P. Thomas) became aware of the fraternity activity is an interesting story.

The society page of the December 16, 1884, edition of the *News and Courier* newspaper in Charleston, S.C., published an account of a party in Columbia, S.C. of Sigma Alpha Epsilon chapters including The Citadel chapter. The account read;

"For several days past, the streets have been enlivened by cadets from the Citadel Academy and the students of South Carolina College have been doing the honors of the city on their behalf. Both the institutions have chapters of Sigma Alpha Epsilon fraternity. Last night, after the exercises of the Literary Societies were concluded, the members of the Lambda Society, the chapter of the South Carolina Military Academy, were invited by the Delta Chapter of the College to the Grand Central Hotel where a handsome supper had been prepared in their honor.

The banquet was presided over by Mr. John A. Rice, who, in an opening address extended a warm welcome to the Citadel chapter. A reply of thanks was made by Cadet J.M. Gibbes. During the evening the following toasts were offered and responded to: "The Fraternity at Large". F. W. Weston; "Grand Chapter", James Hamilton; "Lambda", E.D. Smith; "Theta", B.F. Wilson; "Epsilon of Long Ago", J.M. Haoot; "South Carolina", W.D. Douglas; "State Associations", John Capers; "The Ladies", B.C. Jennings, Wm. McGowan, W.E. Gonzales; " The News and Courier", W.E. Gonzales and W. H Thomas.

The party did not break up until the small hours of the night, and it is a commendable fact that although there was no scarcity of wine, temperance was strictly regarded, and out of thirty five young men, not one lost his way home. This, however, may be in some degree due to the presence of a student brother from the Theological Seminary."

One can only imagine the reaction of Superintendent Thomas and The Citadel administration when they read this account of rowdy

cadet behavior in the local newspaper.

The very next day, December 17, 1884, Colonel Thomas took action in the form of a memorandum to General Johnson Hagood, Chairman of the Board of Visitors. *(Authors note: I am deeply indebted to Major Steve Smith, who not only found the following correspondence in the Citadel Archives, but was able to decipher these 132 year old, hand- written, decaying letters)*

Gen. Hagood   *Dec. 17, 1884*
Chairman, Bd. Vst,

Sir,

I enclose herewith extract from the News and Courier in which the Chairman will recognize credible evidence of the information given by me to the Board at its last meeting of the probable establishment of Secret Colleges Societies in this Academy. I have further two communications addressed to Cadet Smith which seem to point to the same. Not only is this thing a violation of the regulations, but it was explicitly forbidden by me after I read in the present letter received by me of the existence of secret societies in the Corps. While I took no action and did not assume the fact, yet, I took action to inform the Corps against its violation. The following Cadets figure in the societies reported in the News and Courier: J.M. Gibbes, E.D. Smith, B.C. Jennings, J. Capers. I consider it my duty to recommend stringent measures. As the matter seems properly in the realm of the Board from your remarks to me to report further if reports could be confirmed, I will await orders. I believe harm has already been done. My experience leads me to emphasize the utter inconsistency of the secret societies of colleges and Universities with the genius of a military school like this, The (illegible) pledge strikes at the root of our system and more or less unnerves every cadet invested with authority from sentinel on post to Cadet Officer of the Day.

I am yours respectfully.
J. P. Thomas, Supt.

Theta Second Chapter: 1883 - 1885

Apparently, General Hagood, as Chairman, then asked Colonel Thomas to send him written recommendations. In a letter dated some days later, Colonel Thomas wrote to General Hagood;

Dec. 22, 1884

Sir,

Here the basis of an extract from the Columbia (paper) of December 17th enclosed herewith from which it appears that Cadets Gibbes, Capers, B. C. Jennings and E. D. Smith are members of a chapter of a Secret College Society in this Academy. I hereby charge these Cadets with violation of the 192nd Article of the Regulations and with disregard of the special warning of the Supt. On the subject given early in November last in an address to the Corps in which I gave a plain exposition of the law on the subject of unauthorized Cadet Societies with the elements of pledge and secrecy.

I have the honor to make this report prior to the investigation agreeable to the instructions received. I have only to add that the newspaper report seems to confirm the private information which I before received. I have reason to believe that there were five or six of these Secret Societies when I gave my warning and that all promptly disbanded at the time with the exception it appears of the Chapter represented by the Cadets named.

Trusted by the Chairman to give my views as Supt. on the subject, I can only repeat the approbation that these Secret College Societies are wholly at variance with our military methods. Not only do they lend to the formation of petty cliques among Cadets and to the impairment of the unity of the Corps, but what is even more serious the element of Society pledges and obligations seriously affects our whole system of discipline structure based as it is upon the (illegible) Cadets with official (illegible) matters both small and great. Under the auspices of Secret Societies, as I construe them to exist among students the Cadet military arm is more

or less harmonized with the soldiers sense of duty weakened and perverted.

In my judgment the Cadets named in this report, if found guilty after a hearing, deserve such punishment as the Board may direct for what now seems as willful and persistent violations of law. As for evil (illegible) I trust that the Board will deem it wise not only to eradicate it but to provide against its recurrence by a strong penalty. Of course, the Supt. would have these Cadets heard from before any action by the Board upon the charges made.

Yours respectfully,

J.P. Thomas, Supt.

Whether Theta chapter actually surrendered its charter at this time is doubtful, but during 1885-1886 there was no known fraternity activity by Theta. The fraternity of 13 members simply went further underground.

In spite of being sub rosa, the Corresponding Secretary of Theta continued to perform his duty of reporting information to the national headquarters. We have no record of who the Corresponding Secretary was that sent in the first reports of chapter activity in the 1883-1886 timeframe.

Volume II, issue No.1 of *The Kappa Alpha Journal*, published in November, 1884 gives the first public information on the Theta chapter with the following news.

"Kenneth Gordon Matheson '86 is Adjutant of The Citadel Corps of Cadets

Paul Hout Tamplet is cashier of R. E. Fraser's banking house in Georgetown, S.C. (Authors note: he withdrew from school)

Theta Second Chapter: 1883 - 1885

William Edward Dick '86 is Sergeant Major of the Corps of Cadets

Frank Ovid Spain '86 is Captain of Company B of the Citadel Corps of Cadets

William Jennings '86 is First Lieutenant of Company B, Corps of Cadets.

Thomas Perrin Harrison '86 is First Lieutenant of Company A, Quartermaster and First Honor Graduate of his class."

It is obvious from this list that the first initiates of Theta were chosen well. With the exception of Paul Hout Tamplet, who apparently had withdrawn from school before 1885, all occupied high positions of leadership at the school. And it is apparent that the chapter was pleased with their accomplishments.

This same issue contained the names of all the initiates of Theta Second. These men are listed presumably in the order in which they were initiated. They were:

"William Edward Dick, Class of 1886, Sumter, S.C.

Frank Ovid Spain, Class of 1886, Darlington, S.C.

Paul Hout Tamplet, Class of 1886, Georgetown, S.C. (not now in college)

William Jennings, Class of 1886, Charleston, S.C.

Armstrong Jolly Howard, Class of 1886, Effingham, S.C.

Kenneth Gordon Matheson, Class of 1886, Cheraw, S.C.

Thomas Perrin Harrison, Class of 1886, Bradley, S.C.

George Morrall Gadsden, Class of 1886, Charleston, S.C.

Knights of the Order

Benjamin Munnerlyn, Class of 1886, Georgetown, S.C.

Edward Frost Parker, Class of 1886, Charleston, S.C.

Francis Parker Huger, Class of 1887, Charleston, S.C.

Council Black Ashley, Class of 1887, Ellenton, S.C.

Evander McIver Law, Class of 1886, Yorkville, S.C."

Volume III, issue No. 3 of The *Kappa Alpha Journal* published in December, 1885 contains the second reference to Theta chapter members.

It reported that,

"Kenneth Gordon Matheson, '86, was studying law at Cheraw, S.C. and that Paul H. Tamplet, '86 was a cashier at R.E. Fraser's banking house at Georgetown, S.C."

───────────────

Endnotes

1. Chick, *History and Catalogue of the Kappa Alpha Fraternity*, Nashville, Tenn. 1891. P. 124.

2. Smith, *Alumni News*, 2013.

3. Chick, p.124

XIII.
Theta Second Chapter: 1885-1890

A fraternity, like any other organization, goes through phases. As a startup, it faced organizational challenges such as: having a sufficiently large enough core group of members, developing bylaws and governance rules, money enough to support its activities, and elected officers who were diligent in performing their duties. Due to the fact that college is only a four year experience, fraternities faced the constant need to replenish their ranks with good men every year just to keep itself alive.

Communications, both between the chapter and the fraternity headquarters, as well as between the chapter and its members must have been challenging in a *sub rosa* environment. Written documents, within the chapter, if discovered, could be incriminating.

Doing all the above in a sub rosa environment must have been very difficult. Just finding a place for 10-15 men to meet in secret on a closely guarded and regulated military post would have been very difficult.

As noted elsewhere, in those early days, communications between fraternity headquarters and the individual chapters were few and far between. Given these difficulties, it is understandable that Theta chapter would have it ups and down. That it survived and prospered until 1890 is nothing less than a miracle. Its survival is a testament to those men who launched the chapter in 1883, as well as to those 43 men who stood in its ranks from 1883-1890.

From 1885 to 1886, as noted earlier, Theta chapter was inactive. No reports were sent to the Journal. No new members were initiated. It is assumed that chapter meetings, if held at all were infrequent. During the summer of 1886, all of the 13 original members graduated, or

left school except Cadet Council Black Ashley, class of 1887.

The class of 1886 was an exceptional one. It was composed of the three founding members from 1883, as well as those initiated later. These eight original men must have known that they had done something special in creating Theta Chapter, because they decided to have a photograph made of just that group. With the help of the Citadel archivists, and after much research, the following photograph was discovered of that distinguished group. We can now put faces on the names of the three founding members, W.E. Dick, P.H. Tamplet and F.O. Spain as well as the other members of this famous first class.

Members of Kappa Alpha Order in the Citadel graduating class of 1886. Left to Right: T.P. Harrison, G.M. Gadsden, F.O. Spain, K.G. Matheson, A.J. Howard, P.H. Tamplet, William Jennings, W.E. Dick.

Courtesy: The Citadel Archives & Museum, Charleston, South Carolina.

Theta Second Chapter: 1885 - 1890

By the beginning of the school year in October, 1886, the Corps of Cadets had shrunk to 103 men.

By the fall of 1886, apparently the pressures against fraternities had declined. Cadet Ashley undertook to resurrect Theta chapter. Fortunately, he had a valuable and influential ally. Thomas Perrin Harrison, Second Honor Graduate in the class of 1886, was now an Assistant Professor of English at the Citadel. Professor Harrison joined with Cadet Ashley, now a member of the senior class, to select eleven men from the corps for initiation. Six of these men were initiated into the Order on the night of February 18, 1887. Cadet Ashley was assisted in this initiation by George Alexander Norwood, G. H. Edwards, and John Wilkins Norwood. A week later, on the 25th of February, the remaining men were initiated. These men were all members of the fourth class, enrolled in October, 1886 and who would be graduating in the summer of 1890. There were a total of 65 men in the fourth class of the cadet corps at the time, so Theta recruited 15 of the 65.

Volume IV, No. 8 of *The Kappa Alpha Journal*, published in May-June, 1887 contained the following news on Theta Second.

"Armstrong Jolly Howard '86 was teaching at Mars Bluff, S.C.

Thomas Perrin Harrison '86 was assistant instructor of English at The Citadel, Charleston, S.C.

Kenneth Gordon Matheson was instructor of Military Tactics and Commandant of the Corps of Cadets at the South Georgia A and M. College at Milledgeville, GA.

William Edward Dick, the only married man of the chapter was clerking at Sumter, S.C."

Calliopean Literary Society, The Citadel, ca. 1887,

Courtesy: The Citadel Archives & Museum, Charleston, South Carolina.

The Calliopean Literary Society was a literary and debating club originally founded at Yale University in 1819. The Calliopean Literary Society was one of two such societies authorized at The Citadel in the 1880's, the other being the Polytechnic Society. Members of Kappa Alpha Order vied with the other fraternities on campus for offices in these societies.

Volume V, No. 2 of *The Kappa Alpha Journal* published in January, 1888, contained the following report on Theta Second. We can assume that this report was written by Cadet William (Billy) Woodward Dixon, who was the IV, (Corresponding Secretary).

Theta Second Chapter: 1885 - 1890

"Our beloved chapter, Phoenix —like , has risen from its ashes as it were, to which it had been reduced by the separation of its members for a time, while on vacation this summer, and once again is reunited and stands before us strong and full of life and vigor.

With the opening of the academic session in October, there came to us, among the new cadets, some of whom we found to be well qualified in every respect to join with us, and we have spoken to them on the subject, and they seem willing to assume the sacred vows of our fraternity. Some of these gentlemen were recommended to us by a brother of another chapter.

Below, I give a list of the names of our newly-elected officers:

(1) A. G. Singletary, (2) J.L. Ferguson, (3) H.C. Moore, (4) W.W. Dixon, (5) W.E. Mikell, (6) R.W. Hutson, (7) W.H. Simons.

These men are all well qualified to fill the positions entrusted to them.

We received, through Brother W.W. Dixon, printed pamphlets giving a full account of the proceedings at the recent Convention held in Columbia in September. We were glad to see that some changes had been made, and new resolutions adopted, which we highly approve of.

Our chapter is composed of new men comparatively, our oldest member, C. B. Ashley, having graduated last July.

Brother Norwood was instrumental in a great measure in helping us to reorganize our chapter last year, and we owe much of our success to his exertions."

These new members of Theta were both young and inexperienced in the operation of a fraternal organization. No doubt, Cadet Council Black Ashley did what he could to develop the chapter before he graduated in the summer of 1887. Likewise, Professor Harrison probably lent his experience and knowledge to guiding the new men.

The Catalogue of 1891, looking back, reports

"The material was good, but the men lacked knowledge and counsel and an inter-change of ideas with those of large experience and broad views. There was delay in procuring the constitution and ritual and during the first year no Journals were received. Besides these disadvantages, the fact that the chapter was sub rosa kept it confined, checked and deprived of the advantages of freedom."

It is important to note that for the very first time, Theta chapter now had a full complement of officers. For the resurrection of the chapter, they expressed appreciation to both Cadet Council Black Ashley and Brother George Alexander Norwood. For the first time since its birth, the chapter sent a delegate to the Kappa Alpha Convention. In this case, it was the 14th Convention held in Columbia, S.C. on September 20-22, 1887. No doubt the delegate, Cadet William Woodward Dixon returned with new ideas and a determination to insure the growth and success of the chapter.

Thus, as the 1887-1888 school year began, Theta chapter was on the upswing. Time would tell if this progress would last.

By late 1887, Theta Chapter had selected another eight men to be invited to join its ranks. They were George Williams Allison, William Benjamin Davis, William Woodward Dixon, Randolph Bradford Dunbar, James Lennerton Ferguson, Richard Woodward Hutson, Beatie Andrew Inglis and George Yuille MacMurphy. At this point Theta Chapter had a total of 23 members. They reported their progress in the March, 1888, *The Kappa Alpha Journal.*

Volume V, Issue No. 3 of *The Kappa Alpha Journal*, published in March, 1888, contained the following report from Theta Second:

"Our chapter is progressing, but slowly. The men whom we asked to join us some time ago have not yet been initiated, but we have at last secured the use of a hall

Theta Second Chapter: 1885 - 1890

and will initiate them Friday, the 17th inst. They are all good men, and we hope will make good fraternity members.

Our semi-annual examinations have just been completed and most of the boys that came out at the head of our classes were KA's. Our fraternity invariably comes out at the head of everything. May she ever continue to do so.

We were much pleased with the January issue of the Journal, and were glad to see that so many chapters contributed letters this time.

The piece entitled "Shall we have sisters" we thought very good indeed, but Theta does not think we should have sisters, for various reasons.

Our chapter, being a small one, labors under many disadvantages, but we hope as soon as we get in some more men to feel stronger and more able to do our share of work toward furthering the grand cause in which we are so zealously working.

The letter of Brother J. A. Williams, published in the Journal, is just such a one as is needed to stir up delinquent chapters. Theta has been rather tardy in this direction, but she hopes to do better in the future.

With best wishes for each and every chapter for success during the coming year, we close with a reluctant goodbye."

Theta chapter did not offer news to the *Journal* for Volume V, Issue No. 4, however they did respond for the next issue. Volume V, issue No. 5 of *The Kappa Alpha Journal*, published in July, 1888, contained the following report on Theta Second. By this time, William Woodward Dixon had been promoted to the position of II (Vice-President) and William Ephriam Mikell had been appointed the IV (Corresponding Secretary).

"Theta, after a long silence of nearly four months, sends greetings to her sister chapters.

Knights of the Order

At our recent election the following were elected; (1) A.G. Singletary, (2) W.W. Dixon, (3) R. B. Dunbar, (4) W.E. Mikell, (5) G.W. Allison, (6) E.R. Zemp, (7 and 8) W.H. Simons. These men are fully competent to hold the offices to which they have been assigned, and under their mild but just rule Theta is certain to prosper. Although we are laboring under a great disadvantage, still old Theta will come out ahead. At our recent picnic, we had three K.A. boys on the committee, which we considered a great honor as they were put there by the vote of the entire school, and were moreover, the only men in their class who secured a place on the committee.

We were also very successful at our competitive drill, as Brother Dunbar obtained the medal for being the best drilled man in the corps. Bro. Dixon also received a medal for being the best drilled man in his company. Bros. Singletary and Mikell were highly honored by being selected to write the essays for their respective literary societies at the annual debate, which took place the first of June. It is needless to say that they both were very highly complimented on their essays and old Theta was proud of them.

Then again for our commencement exercises, five K.A's have been chosen by the professors to speak; they are: Bros. Singletary, Dunbar, Dixon, Mikell and Magrauth. Bro. Dixon, or "Billy", as the boys call him, has the reputation of breaking more hearts than any other fellow in the corps.

We were also pleased with the last number of the Journal; it seems to grow better at each issue; we certainly have the right kind of men at the head of it. We are also greatly in favor of the certificate of membership plan as advocated in our last Journal, as each member could have one framed and hung up in his home, and it will help to bring to his mind many pleasant recollections of years gone by; we are also in favor of something neat and pretty in the way of charter permits on parchment. Theta has been so successful in the last four months and failing to get a letter in the last Journal, she could write a long epistle, but as our space in the Journal is limited we will close with an affectionate adieu."

Theta Second Chapter: 1885 - 1890

This report in the *Journal* is important for a number of reasons.

1. It proves the chapter had a full complement of officers.

2. It refers to the "great disadvantage" the fraternity has, being *sub rosa* and confirms this was a problem.

3. It highlighted the many talented leaders in Theta chapter.

4. It expressed the chapter's obvious pride in its members.

5. It supported the efforts underway to get each member a certificate of membership suitable for framing.

6. It confirmed that chapter charters of the time were hand-written and advocated a change from chapter charters being handwritten to more formal printed charters on parchment.

Things changed as the chapter matured and by the 1888-1889 school years, Theta Chapter was clearly prospering. The 1891 Catalogue again reports,

"A knowledge of the proper operations of chapters and their relation to the Order at large was gradually absorbed by the members through contact with men from other chapters and after the first year, the Journal. All this time the foundation was being laid for a future career of usefulness and distinction. Though in a manner crippled by the difficulties of its position, the chapter made good use of its opportunities and made itself felt in the institution, more honors being distributed among her members than among any of the other fraternities represented at the academy."

The 1891 Catalogue further detailed the progress being made with this report.

"The session of 1888-1889 opened under conditions very favorable to the chapter. A compete system of bylaws was drafted and adopted, more system was observed, meetings were regularly held, the proceedings of which were carefully kept, business of importance was transacted and new life and interest developed in the members. The officers were strict in their attention to duty and watchful of the interests committed to their keeping."

The next Theta report is found in the March, 1889 Journal. Volume VI, Issue No. 3, of *The Kappa Alpha Journal* contained the following report on Theta. This report was undoubtedly written by Cadet Mikell, the IV.

"At last, the excitement of the semi-annual examination is over, and as was expected, Theta's men have done credit to themselves and to the chapter. Brother Simons will continue to "hold the fort" at the head of the class, which place he has held for three consecutive years, and will without doubt, graduate a la tete. Brother Allison stands fourth. There are others who stand well, but our limited space will not permit their names to appear in this issue. Suffice it to say, that in the third class we claim the second, third and fifth places, besides others a little lower down, and in the fourth class, the ninth place and one more lower down. So much for class standing.

It is with great pleasure that I now introduce to the fraternity at large Brothers E. Mikell Whaley, James Frances McElwee and Newton Pinckney Walker. These men stand well in their classes and in the estimation of the school, and are worthy to be joined in heart to us by every tie of fraternal love.

For the last month we have been lamenting the loss of one of our best men, Brother Dunbar. Much too our sorrow, he was called home under certain un-avoidable circumstances, and will not be able to return. Just about the time this brother left us the outlooks of Theta were very unpropitious, and the departure of Brother Dunbar has made it more so; but I'm glad to say it did not remain this way any length of time, for, all at once, we determined to revolutionize things,

so every man by putting his shoulder to the wheel, helped raise Theta out of a mire that she will not get in again directly; no, not if the court knows itself, and I think it does. We have now adopted a complete set of bylaws, besides several other necessaries which we cannot mention here. We have, as it were, passed from childhood to manhood.

A contest between the two literary societies is to take place soon. Brothers Dixon and Lake have been selected for debaters, with Brother Mikell as declaimer by one of the societies, while Brother Singletary has been elected orator by the other.

Since our last letter was written there have been two new chapters established here-one of the ΛΤΩ *and the other* ΠΚΛ. *They both have our very best wishes. The* ΛΤΩ *chapter is an old friend of ours, but like Theta, she was unfortunate and fell, but after several years rose again, and it is with kindest feelings that we welcome her, and wish her the greatest success.*

We now have in school only forty fraternity men, divided as follows; ΛΤΩ, *6,* ΣΑΕ, *7,* ΣΝ, *17,* ΚΑ, *13,* ΠΚΑ, *4.*(Authors note: no explanation for why these numbers do not total forty)

Wishing all of our sister societies much success in the coming term. We close with an affectionate adieu."

This report, issued in the middle of the 1888-1889 school year is very positive and upbeat. The competition for grades, rank and school committee assignments continued. Three new men were inducted and there were laments at losing Cadet Dunbar. With the adoption of new bylaws, the Corresponding Secretary described the status of the chapter as going from "childhood to manhood". It is also evident that fraternity activity was expanding throughout the school with five active fraternities.

This March, 1889 issue of *The Kappa Alpha Journal* also contained a list of Theta's 1888 initiates and their date of initiation.

Knights of the Order

"Robert Brodie Jones, Savannah, GA., February 17, 1888

Beattie Andrew Inglis, Madison, FL., February 17, 1888 (Authors note: This is a mistake by the Corresponding Secretary. Brother Inglis was initiated in 1887. This should contain the name of Brother John Finlayson Mays, Jefferson County, FL.)

Joseph Walker Magrath, Charleston, S.C., February 17, 1888

Thomas Joab Mauldin (address not given), June 22, 1888

John Lake, Edgefield, S.C., June 22, 1888

Newton Pinckney Walker, Spartanburg S.C., December 14, 1888

James Frank McElwee, Yorkville, S.C., December 14, 1888

Ephraim Mikell Whaley, Edisto Island, S.C., December 14, 1888"

Thus by the end of 1888, the original 15 members from 1887 had been joined by 8 others for a total of 23 members initiated by Theta Second chapter since its resurrection in 1887.

Volume VI, issue No. 4 of *The Kappa Alpha Journal* was published in May, 1889. It contained the following report from the Theta Second Chapter, At this point, Cadet Mikell had been promoted to the II (Vice-President) and Cadet John Lake had been appointed the IV or Corresponding Secretary. It begins with a poem.

"The spring is here-the delicate-footed May

With its slight fingers full of leaves and flowers"

"It is true. Spring has indeed dawned on us with all its loveliness, and with it comes a thirst to waste in wood-paths its voluptuous hours. The trees have all put on the spring suits of a pretty green color, and a few straw hats may be seen

Theta Second Chapter: 1885 - 1890

bobbing up and down in the motley crowd on King Street. Picnics are on a boom here. The Cadet picnic is to come off on the 3rd of May. Brother Singletary has been elected by the corps to be on one of the committees. He was the only man we (K.A.s) tried to get on.

Theta had quite a treat last month in the way of an elegant little supper, tendered us by Brother Magrath in honor of three of our members, who very recently came of age. The fair sex predominated and had everything pretty much their own way. The supper-room was a sight worth seeing, one of its specialties being the decorations on the windows, which were very artistically arranged, with the mystic letters, K.A. hanging gracefully over them. These letters were worked in the colors of our fraternity by one of Charleston's prettiest and most graceful maidens. Brother Magrath has the thanks of our entire chapter, for everyone had a royal time, and it is only modesty that keeps us from telling him to "call again".

We are almost ready for the convention. (Authors Note: This would be the 15th Convention held on September 11-13, 1889 in Augusta, Ga.) *Brother Mikell has been elected to represent us at that time, and as required, he will be instructed with the desires and suggestions of this chapter. We feel certain that it is going to be meeting worth going to and of great benefit to the order.*

We were very much pleased with our last Journal, but we were very sorry to see that so few of our alumni subscribe to it. We sincerely hope that they will do better in the future.

We are all very busy at present getting ready for the competitive drill which is to take place on the 24th of May. It will be remembered that two of Theta's men won prizes for being the best drilled men in their respective companies last year, and we stand a pretty good chance this year.

Fraternity news here is very scarce. We have made no other initiates and I don't think any of the other fraternities have either. There is generally a feeling of friendship among all, and I hope it will continue. With these words my letter ends."

It is evident that the arrival of the spring of 1889 stirred the poetry in Cadet Lake's heart. He waxed eloquent in his description of the spring time weather, the elaborate dinner enjoyed by the chapter and the beautiful, local maidens.

Volume VI, issue No. 5 of *The Kappa Alpha Journal*, published in July, 1889 contained the following report on Theta Chapter.

"Once more it is my privilege to write Theta's chapter letter, and to offer to our sister chapters our mite of good, bad and indifferent news. As I still hold the honorable position of C.S., having been elected for a second term, I hope to chronicle many more laurels won and to add many more worthy names to our role, so that when I shake off this mortal coil of S.C.M.A. life and lay down my pen to be succeeded by a more worthy quill driver, I shall have the satisfaction of leaving our much beloved chapter in a flourishing and permanent condition.

In looking back over the past year, we cannot but smile with satisfaction over what has been accomplished. Our chapter is now in the best condition it ever was in, and our men deserve credit for the faithfulness with which they have fulfilled their offices and for the energy and good spirit which they threw in their work. And so it ought to be, not only in our own little chapter, but throughout the whole fraternity. Brethren, we've got one of the finest fraternities in the South. Let us make it the best in the United States. What say you? It can be done. If we (all the brethren) say so, it will be done. Come one and come all. Let us pull "with a strong, strong pull and a pull altogether", and raise Kappa Alphaism up to and over the very highest rung in the ladder, so that ere long the very highest and greatest compliment that can be paid to son of man will be to say, "He is a Kappa Alpha."

At our last election, the following officers were: (1 and 8) W.H. Simons, (2) W.E. Mikell, (3 John Lake, (4 and 7) W.W. Dixon, (5) G.W. Allison, (6) E.R. Zemp, (9) A.G. Singletary. These brothers are fully competent to hold their respective offices, so under their rule, we have a very bright future before us.

Theta Second Chapter: 1885 - 1890

Our annual hop is to come off the 28ᵗʰ of this month. It is given by the second class in honor of our graduates here. Every K.A. in the second class was elected to serve on some committee. Brother Singletary has been elected chairman. Our hop this year promises to be one of the most successful we have ever had.

We were very glad to learn that our next Convention is to be held in Augusta, as we think that is decidedly the best place. We are looking for much good to come from this Convention, but we hope no such changes as will affect our alumni will be made, such as grips and countersigns.

There has recently been organized here a glee club for the instruction and amusement of the members, but I notice with pleasure that it has brought men of different fraternities into closer friendship and in doing that it has accomplished no little thing.

We all go up to Greenville on the encampment the first part of next month, and we hope to see some of Iota's (Furman University) boys. As we will not be able to get to them, we hope they will come to see us. I am sure they will always be welcomed in camp.

We are all very busy now getting ready for examination, and as the time comes for us to leave we all have to go to our best girl and breathe many a sweet vow of fidelity as we received our badges, and as we —but guess I had better leave the rest to the imagination of our many brothers, for I fear our girls mightn't like it. With these remarks, I close. Let us come back next term, dear brothers, with a firm desire to do our duty both to our fraternity and fellowmen."

This report would have been the last one for the 1888-1889 school year which ended in July, 1889. Cadet John Lake is still the Corresponding Secretary and he appears to be very satisfied with the position Theta Second Chapter is in. He calls it the "best condition it ever was in." He then follows with a pep talk to his audience, the other chapters, about making Kappa Alpha the "best (fraternity) in the

Knights of the Order

United States." It appears that the fraternity has a full complement of officers. The General Convention of 1889 to be held in Augusta, Ga. was eagerly anticipated. Cadet Lake closes with a challenge to his brethren to return in the fall ready to go back to work for "our fraternity and our fellowmen."

The Citadel ca. 1886
Courtesy: The Citadel Archives & Museum, Charleston, SC

October, 1889 was the beginning of the last school year for the original 15 Theta members of the Class of 1890. Unknown to the members of Theta, it was to be the last school year for the formal existence of Theta Second Chapter. However, the new school year began on a very positive note.

Volume VII, Issue No.2 of *The Kappa Alpha Journal* published in November, 1889 contained the following report on Theta. It is assumed that Cadet Lake is still the Corresponding Secretary.

"Theta sends to her sister chapters greetings and wishes for each and every one a bright, successful and happy session.

We have reopened under the brightest of prospects, and have a large, new class, full of good fraternity material, from which to select, and our now full ranks will soon to be overflowing. Just before we closed last year we initiated into the mysteries of our sacred order, Brother P.K. McCully, of Anderson, S.C. and on October

19, 1889, Brother R. B. Grier, of Yorkville, S.C. had the grip for the first time extended to him. Both of these brothers are good and enthusiastic K.A.'s and are worthy to be bound to us by every tie of fraternal love. The will both no doubt, win many a laurel for old Theta.

We have the honor of claiming the first three officers in the school, besides other good ones. Brother Singletary is Captain of Company A. Brother Dixon of D, and Brother Simons is Adjutant of the corps. Brother Mikell is a Lieutenant, while Brothers Mauldin, Lake, Robertson, Whaley and McCully all hold the office of Sergeants. Besides these, we have other officers lower down, but for the want of room they must be omitted.

We rejoice with exceeding great joy over the success of our last convention. She was a hard hit to center, good for three bags, sure. The changes that were made are all for the best, so we can all look out for a most brilliant career before us.

We all ought to work together to gain one end now- the advancement and perfection of Kappa Alphaism. Now is the time to act, while we are enthused and have new blood in our veins. We can write enthusiastic letters, full of vim and spirit, and thus stir up the men of our own and other chapters.

Theta has lots of hard work before her this year, for her strongest foothold is in the first class, so when they graduate, they want to leave their chapter in the hands of live and energetic men. They also want it to be in a permanently flourishing condition, and this can only be obtained by making it stronger in the lower classes.

There are still five fraternities in the school, and I am happy to say that the very friendliest feelings exist between them all.

The Glee Club is still on the go, and is the source of much amusement. It has been the instrument of bringing the fraternities in close communion with each other, hence friendliness follows.

With a God-speed on your journey to our sisters, we now close our letter and long

for the time when our Journal shall appear."

THE REPORT CONTINUED.....

"Theta did not get a letter in the last Journal, for the reason that the C.S. was not notified of the change made in the time for issuing of the Journal, until sometime after the specified time for sending on the letter.

We were very much struck with the first number of our new Journals. It shows that the men we have running it are not only competent, but fully determined to do their work well. Just look at this last (No. 1). Although it had so few letters in it, still it was full to overflowing with good and very interesting literature. And if it is that good now, what will it not be when it gets a good, strong support from the chapters and alumni?

Theta has some hard work before her this year, but she is equal to the occasion, and those men who graduate intend to do their best to leave her in good health and strength. We are not fast workers. We believe firmly in that saying, "an ounce of prevention is worth a pound of cure", so we go around with our eyes wide open and when we get a man we generally know him.

There is one marked distinction among "our" boys here. Take them collectively or individually, and they are all given to sentimentality, from Billy Simons up to the C.S. We know Billy is in love; as for the C.S. —well, I'll keep silent, but I "know my number."

"Let's have the Catalogue as soon as possible", is our next cry. This has been a long —felt want, and we rejoice to see that we are going to have it soon." (Authors Note: This refers to the Directory and Catalogue, finally published in 1891).

"Theta's boys seem to have a peculiar charm for attracting the fair maidens of this city. One of Charleston's sweetest and very prettiest young ladies requested us to hold our last meeting at her house, which we did and were cordially invited to do so again. This is only one case out of a hundred which we might bring up to prove

Theta Second Chapter: 1885 - 1890

the popularity of "our boys" with the fair sex here. And so it should be everywhere we have chapters, for are they not dearer to us than others?

Both fraternity news and material are scarce around these diggings. Out of a new class of seventy, there are scarcely twenty- five good men.

We are trying for a banquet Christmas, and our many lady fiends are made happy over the idea, for they know what it is to "be there".

With the very best wishes for the success of our sister chapters, I say in the words of an Irishman, "bon sour"."

The above report again emphasized the quality of the men in Theta. Two of the four cadet companies were commanded by Theta men (Archibald Gilchrist Singletary and William Woodward Dixon). The Adjutant (William Howe Simons) of the Corps was a Theta man along with other officers and underclassmen with rank. There is a reference to the success of the Convention and an excitement about Kappa Alpha. It was noted that there were still five fraternities active on the Citadel campus that fall of 1889.

As we have seen in several of the reports, the Theta men enjoyed the company of the lovely young ladies of Charleston and obviously competed with the other men of the corps for their attention.

Finally, it was observed that the new class of 70 plebes did not impress the Theta men. They observed that scarcely 25 of them were fraternity material. Whether this was the standard prejudice of an upperclassman's views of new fourth classmen is unknown.

Volume VII, issue No. 3 of *The Kappa Alpha Journal*, published in December, 1889, contained the following report on Theta Second. Again, the Corresponding Secretary begins with a poem.

Knights of the Order

"That men may say, when we the front box grace,
Behold the first in virtue as in face."

Theta sends greetings to her sister chapters and hopes they have been as successful in the last month as she has. We now have a chapter that will compare favorably with any other. We have eighteen of the handsomest and most clever men in the school, with the exception of the C.S., and we are going to do some splendid work this session.

Since our last letter we have added two worthy names to our roll- Brothers W. B. Daniels and C.L. O'Neal, whom I now introduce to the fraternity at large. Both of the brothers are made of the best material, and will, without doubt, be an honor not only to our chapter but to the whole fraternity.

Theta holds a "royal straight flush" in one hand and a "full house" in the other with the fair sex of this city. Compliment after compliment has been showered on us by them, and it is a great wonder that we are not conceited(?).

The last treat tendered to us was a magnificent K.A. lunch. This was through the extreme kindness of Brother Magrath and for which he has the manifold thanks of the chapter. Six of Charleston's "beauties" took the part of "garcons" with a grace that was entrancing in itself. It is said that Brother Mikell was so confused at the sight that he ate seven plates of salad. "It was really a most remarkable scene."

For reasons unknown we failed to get our last number of the Journal. This was indeed a bitter disappointment. We always look forward to the coming of this little volume with the greatest of pleasure, and it always fills our veins with new blood. We hope we will not be overlooked again.

We are busy now preparing for what is always regarded by us a "big thing"-our Christmas hop. Theta has four men serving on the committee, only seniors serving on the committees. This hop promises to be one of the finest ever given here. Hundreds of dollars are being spent in the preparation of this coming festival, and the

Theta Second Chapter: 1885 - 1890

old citadel will undergo a complete transformation.

Fraternity news is scare but fraternity material is scarcer still. Out of a new class of sixty odd men there is hardly any fraternity material at all.

We have at last decided to run the risk and procure a chapter hall as soon as possible. Being sub rosa, it is right risky to get a hall in a very public place, but we are going to run the gauntlet, and if we perish, we perish. There is one thing certain. With a chapter as large as ours, a chapter hall is almost absolutely essential for the welfare of the chapter; and this way of having our meetings at different places, like an Arab, doesn't suit us at all.

Thetas sends seven young men out in the world to scratch for themselves this coming June. They are all very sorry to leave, but have the satisfaction of knowing that they leave their dear old chapter in good hands, and that it is in a permanent, prosperous condition. This sweetens to a high degree the bitterness of our cup.

A joint debate is to take place soon between the two literary societies here. Brothers Singletary and Mikell have been appointed debaters, and Brother Magrath one of the orators of the occasion.

With best wishes for our sister chapters, we close. In the words of the tonsorial artist, "Next."

This report expands on the last one seeking to establish that Theta is in excellent shape. They now have 18 members and have added Brothers William Bicell Daniels and Charles Livingston O'Neal to the ranks. They still are also focused on one of the main preoccupations of young men—girls. Describing themselves as holding a "royal straight flush" in one hand and a "full house" in the other when it comes to the fair sex, they seem to be on top of the world. Apparently, they are holding regular events, including a lunch complete with young ladies present.

On a more somber note, they have decided to run the risk of obtaining a chapter hall. Where that chapter hall was located is not known. They recognize their sub rosa status and the dangers presented by going public. Nevertheless, they have decided to press on, ending their past practice of moving from meeting place to meeting place "like an Arab". This was certainly a courageous decision, but one that more than likely contributed to their demise a year later.

Seven of the men who entered in the fall of 1886 were scheduled to graduate in June of 1890, but they were satisfied that the chapter was in good shape and being left in good hands.

Volume VII, issue No. 4 of *The Kappa Alpha Journal*, published in January, 1890, contains the following report on Theta Second.

"As we look back over the year just past, a flood of sweet recollections sweeps over us and we cannot help but turn our hearts to Him who rules over us and pour out our heart-felt thanks for the manifold mercies which he has showered upon us. It is true that with the good there has been mingled some bad, but the latter has been but a background with which to bring out the brightest colors of the former.

Dear old Theta has had her share of both. At times, when struggling in the storm of life, her masts would be bent so far as to touch the water, but it was only to rise again to ride more gracefully on the waves.

Theta has had some very heavy demands on her financial department, which were unavoidable; so she is not exactly up on her dues. It was not, however, from a want of enthusiasm of loyalty that the dues were not paid, but it was because of more pressing demand just at that time. This will soon be obliterated though and I am sure we will not get behind again. It is not old Theta who would stand idle and see her brethren bear the expenses and do all the work, while she shares the fruits and glory of their toiling.

It gives me great pleasure to introduce to our order at large Brother J.R. Hart.

Theta Second Chapter: 1885 - 1890

This brother's name was omitted in our last by an oversight. It is needless to discuss this brother's worthiness, for he has already proven to us what he really is, and although at a minimum in stature, he is above par in intellect.

One of the most brilliant and successful events in the social world here took place on the evening of the 26th of December, 1889, and was in the form of a hop, given by the Cadets of the S.C M.A. It was pronounced by one and all to have been the most successful hop ever given by the Cadets. As stated before Theta had four men on the committees, only seniors serving, and they all worked hard. We had the pleasure of having some of our brothers from Rho with us at the time, and we truly say we were exceedingly glad to have them with us. We only regret that we could not have had more of our brethren with us.

Talk about fraternity magazines, what's the matter with the Journal? It is indeed like a drink of cool water to a tired, thirsty traveler. And although other fraternities have decided that is it almost impossible to keep up a monthly, still we will show them that Kappa Alpha can even overcome impossibilities.

With best wishes for our sister chapters, we close."

The report for the fateful year of 1890 began on a mixed note in January. Theta was having some financial trouble caused by dues being in arrears. They initiated another cadet, apparently in late 1889, John Ratchford Hart.

Formal dances at The Citadel were known as "hops" and sponsored by the school. There was one on the evening of December 26, 1889, described as "the most successful one ever given by the cadets". They also noted that brothers from the Rho (University of South Carolina) chapter attended the dance.

Volume VII, issue No.5 of *The Kappa Alpha Journal*, published in February, 1890 contains the following report from Theta.

Knights of the Order

"The melancholy days have come-The saddest of the year

Still, Theta's members do not seem to be very much "under the weather" for we still hold our heads and positions high as ever. The sad days referred to is examination week, which is now upon us. Although examinations are not especially beloved by us, still we hold our own, and so far our fellows have always done credit to themselves and to their chapter.

Speaking of billy-goats, we have one of the most venerable and sagacious old fellows that is to be found in these parts. While straying in the fields of barbarism, eating all the old tomato cans which they (the barbs) threw at him, he caught sight of Mr. R.N. Perrin. With his usual alacrity he lifted him over the fence into the verdant fields of Kappa Alpha, where peace and concord reign supreme, and where we, with the fear of God and the love for our fellow-men, strive for the "farther strand". I now introduce this brother to the fraternity at large. I will not dwell on his merits; suffice it to say, he stands at the head of a class of fifty six men.

The election of speakers for the two literary societies here resulted in Brother Singletary, Orator; Grier, Valedictorian for the Polytechnic Society; and Brothers Mikell, Valedictorian and Dixon, Debater, for the Calliopean Society. Brother Allison is a Marshal. Brother Simons, as "first honor man" speaks on Commencement Day. Not a K.A. was left out-a record hard to beat and of which we are very proud.

Many a pleasant time we have had in our lives, but the most pleasant was at Brother Magrath's magnificent lunch, which was tendered to the chapter by him last Saturday. Brother Magrath has been so kind to us in this respect, as well as in all others, that if he were to leave us, I really believe we would miss him.

We will give a dance next Friday evening and our lady friends, as well as we, are expecting something extra fine. If we disappoint them, it will be an exception to the general rule; we've got a "rep" in that direction.

"What's everybody's business is nobody's business" and that's the reason Johnny didn't get his hair cut. Such seems to be the case in respect to our much-needed and much-talked of Catalogue. We all feel that we ought to have one, but I don't think any of us exert ourselves very much over this highly-important matter. There is a great demand for this book; other fraternities are ahead of us in this respect. Are we to "bring up the rear", even in this? I think not. We lead, not follow. Therefore, let us push forward this very desirous object with all diligence, for it is high time it was completed.

We notice that there are one or two chapters who never have a word to say in the Journal. What's the matter with these brothers? Is it because the flame of patriotism has died out? We trow not. Still, they might give us a word now and then, for if they have lost all interest in themselves, we have not.

With best wishes for our sister chapters, we close."

This February issue found the cadets in the midst of examinations. Described as the "melancholy days" the members of Theta were determined to hold their own. Apparently it worked because the Corresponding Secretary listed numerous honors for Theta members-in fact, it was noted that "not a Kappa Alpha was left out". The one new initiate, Robert McCaw Perrin, was hailed as the academic leader of his class of 56 men. He was a freshman at that time.

The monthly lunches continued as did the dances. There was criticism of the fraternity headquarters for the delay in producing the catalogue which had been long expected.

The tension between the gentlemen and the "barbs" was evident in another comment disparaging of the non-fraternity men. This tension was to continue and grow in the spring of 1890.

Volume VII, issue No.6 of *The Kappa Alpha Journal*, published in March, 1890, contained the following report on Theta chapter.

Knights of the Order

"Once more Theta sends her wee bit of good, bad and indifferent news to her sister chapters, and sends to each and all of them greetings. The "barbs" here are on the war-path. They received a thrust not long ago which was anything but pleasant, and like a Thomas-cat, whose silken fur having been stoked in the wrong way, raises his majestic terminus and gives vent to his wrath in a tune of four sharps and three flats, they have caused the Greeks to tremble-with laughter. The cause of their capers is this: In the elections for the annual picnic, which takes place in May, the "barbs" were shut out completely. This riled the laddies, for, said they, "We are a party of good men, and deserve to be represented on this committee". Such logic, however, did not suit us, so it only remains for vengeance to be rained down from above on us who have maltreated these innocent ones. We have four men on the committee. The committee is a follows; Kappa Alpha, 4; Alpha Tau Omega, 2; Sigma Alpha Epsilon, 2; Sigma Nu, 5. We have the chairman. The P.K.A's have united with the non-frats. These men were elected by the entire corps.

That old but terrible chestnut, "la grippe" had been raging here for some time, but is about to be checked now. From the effects of the same, brother McCully is home on a sick furlough. The furlough must be sick for I don't think "Pete" is.

Brother Daniels has been honorably discharged on account of sickness and Brother Lake is home also, on account of his eyes. However, this brother hopes to return soon.

As far as I know, there have been no recent initiates in any of the fraternities here. There is peace and harmony among us all, and we are living as we should do- in a friendly relation to each other.

Childbirth most certainly disagrees with our mother, Alpha. Her voice is no longer heard in our midst, and we are left in ignorance of her condition. But we hope this will not continue to be the case. Alpha is the first; shall the first become the last in this case? I think not. In fact, I look for a long letter from her in the very next issue of the Journal." (Authors Note: This refers to the demise of the

Theta Second Chapter: 1885 - 1890

*original Alpha chapter at Washington and Lee University which went under in
1870, but was revived in 1875. It was inactive again from 1878 to 1885. It has
been active since 1885 to the present.)*

*"The respective class standings of the different classes here have been published.
Brother Simons still holds his position as head man of his class (first). The others
have changed very little, so I will not repeat them.*

*Brother Dixon has been highly complimented on his voice. As Captain of Com-
pany "D" like the noise of mighty waters it can be heard from afar.*

*We are glad to hear that a small clew has been found concerning our much-abused
Catalogue. Though it is but a shadow of a shade it's still something. It's a move
in the right direction, and who knows but before very long what is now a phantom
may stand before us in reality?*

With an affectionate adieu and a God-speed on your journey, I close."

Open warfare broke out between the "barbs" and the "Greeks "as
shown in the March, 1890 report. It arose from the competition for
places of honor at the college. Apparently, the men from the fraternities ran their own slate of officers for the Annual Picnic. The entire
corps voted on the men and only fraternity men were elected. Kappa
Alpha had 4 men on the committee of 13—all fraternity men. Even
though the non-fraternity men protested, claiming they deserved
recognition, the fraternity men refused to compromise. In fact, they
mocked the non-fraternity men. This episode, small as it may seem,
may well have been the catalyst that set in motion the final demise of
fraternities among cadets at The Citadel.

Volume VII, issue No. 7 of *The Kappa Alpha Journal*, published in
April, 1890 contained the following report on Theta chapter.

"It becomes my duty to once more send a few words of greeting to our sister chap-

Knights of the Order

ters. *As I begin to write I cannot suppress a feeling of sadness which creeps over me at the thought that I shall never again have the pleasure of writing a letter for dear old Theta in the capacity of her C.S. My term of office expires before the next letter is due, and I with six other brothers, will have finished our course here, and will be sent out into the world to fight for ourselves, to learn of its joys and its sorrows, its pleasures and pains.*

As we realize this fact, we have endeavored to leave our chapter in as strong and as prosperous a condition as possible. So far, we have the very best prospects. We are well satisfied with what we have done. We try not to be presumptuous; we weigh our material carefully, and with a slow but firm tread we are gradually pushing up to the front. We now have seventeen good and energetic men, and if nothing happens to prevent we will commence our next term with the goodly number of ten. We do not hesitate to say that our chapter will flourish, for she will be in the hands of men who are enthusiastic and hard workers and who would do anything in their power for their chapter, - in the plain vernacular, they are K.A.'s.

I sincerely trust that when we leave our chapter, we will not treat her as the majority of her present alumni do. The least they could do would be to support the Journal-that little volume which is almost worth its weight in gold-almost, did I say? Well, I'm wrong, it's a great deal more. As spicy and as fresh as a sea-breeze itself, it puts new life in our bodies, new thoughts in our heads and refreshes to a great extent, in general the inner man. Too much praise cannot be showered upon those who have the management of it; for it is indeed a credit to them as well as to the order for those whose good they are working; and it is to be pitied that they do not receive more practical encouragement than they do.

In the rush and excitement that has prevailed here this year, we have almost forgotten that we are sub rosa. We have thrown off our covering and stood out with a boldness that is next to recklessness. But I do not think this is for the best, for we do not know at what moment we are going to be "sat upon", therefore I think it best to exercise some degree of caution, although we may not see the use of it now.

There has been a great deal of excitement here over the above mentioned picnic election and in consequence of which the school is divided. The Greeks are going to have a picnic of their own, and they have made very elaborate preparations for the same. The Barbs are going to have a sail- a cool sail, 3'oclock in the day. We bear them no malice; we only hope they will enjoy themselves, and I don't doubt but that they will.

We received a curious little package the other day, and for a while were at a loss to account from whence it came. On receiving it, there immediately came across our minds visions of broken vows, side-doors, hen-roosts, policemen, sheriffs, and last the Black Maria. But our fears were soon transformed into joy, for on opening it we found-not a bank note, but our part of the Catalogue, returned to be corrected and re-written in the required form. This was indeed a great surprise, but a very pleasant one. Now let's "whoop her up", and before you know it, presto, change! "right out of this gentleman's hat , sir", and we've got it.

We're sorry to announce the Brother Lake, who we thought, would be able to return to us finds it will be impossible for him to do so. In losing this brother, Theta loses one of her best men. He was looked upon by the entire corps as a true model of truth, purity, nobleness and manhood."

Cadet John Lake, the former Corresponding Secretary, had left school apparently in mid-year and we do not know who took his place for this one report. However, his replacement expresses his sadness in writing the report for the last time. He is graduating in a few months and will be turning over the Corresponding Secretary position to Cadet Peter Keys McCully. The Corresponding Secretary expresses confidence in the future of Theta chapter and notes that they now have 17 good men and after 7 graduated in the summer of 1890, the chapter will begin the October, 1890 school year with 10 brothers.

Unfortunately, the seeds of the demise of Theta had already been

sown. He admits they had "almost forgotten" they were sub rosa. They had thrown off their cover (dances, open meetings, lunches, etc., and admitted that was "reckless." He believes the chapter should show some degree of "caution."

The "picnic election" issue still had not been resolved and apparently the "barbs" decided not to participate in the picnic, but to have an event of their own. No doubt, the officials at The Citadel were well aware of the dissention in the ranks and the division between the "barbs" and the "greeks" among the cadets on campus. Something had to be done.

Finally, the draft of the long-awaited Catalogue arrived for proofreading. This was a source of great delight to the men of Theta Second.

Volume VII, issue No. 8 of *The Kappa Alpha Journal*, published in May, 1890 contained the following report on Theta.

"Tis not without a tremor that I take up my pen for the first time to address the fraternity at large through the pages of the Journal. But I will find something to say if it's only to inform the order at large that Theta is still in existence.

At our last meeting the following officers were installed: (1) E.M. Whorly, (2) T.J. Mauldin, (3) P.K. McCully, (4) J.F. McElwee, (5) J.M. Robertson, (6) J.W. Magrath, (7) R.M. Perrin, (8) J.R. Hart. So the last election in the Calliopean Literary Society Brother Robertson (J.M.) was elected treasurer, and Brother Magrath, Quarterly Orator. On the same night elections took place in the cadet Polytechnic Society, where owing to a strong "barbarian" combination we did not get any offices.

Soon seven of our best men will leave us; all of them graduate well in their class and out of the seven, five will speak at the Commencement. Brother Simons is Valedictorian, as he graduates first in his class of 37 men. At the commencement exercises of the literary societies, Brothers Mikell and Dixon represent the

Calliopean, while Brother Singletary and Grier will speak for the Polytechnic. We have more speakers at Commencement than any other fraternity here.

Alpha Tau Omega has made one initiate since the last issue of the Journal, all the other fraternities are quiet. We will probably not take in any more men this year. Brother E. M. Parker has been with us some time as acting surgeon of the Academy.

Brothers Singletary, Dixon, Simons and Mikell have been much complimented in the way they drilled the battalion when the cadet officers were drilling it by turns. The competitive drill between the four companies and also the drill for the individual prize comes off on May 24. Brother McCully now wears the medal which was awarded to him as the best drilled man in the corps last year. I am certain that Theta's men will distinguish themselves this year, as two companies are commanded by our men, and the rest of the members are practicing continually to try and win the medal away from Brother McCully.

The cadet picnic came off on May 2, and a glorious success it was. Brother Dixon was chairman of the whole committee and Brothers Zemp, Allison and Grier were on the dancing arrangement and invitation committees respectively. All of our boys enjoyed themselves thoroughly, and the crimson and gold was worn by a large number of young ladies present. In fact several were known to take off the colors of another fraternity to don the emblems of K.A. We were delighted to have with us on that occasion several of Rho's (University of South Carolina) members, and also a large number of K.A. Alumni.

The committee wore something novel in the way of badges, shoulder straps, which in several instances had the letters of the fraternity on them and which made a very pretty show on the gray uniforms. Brother John Lake is with us now, and we only wish he could be with us as a cadet again, in him, we lost one of the best men that ever wrestled with Theta's goat.

Brother Grier vanquished the whole corps recently. He sang one verse of a song

93

and everyone started out with the intention of killing him. Undaunted by the terrible array drawn up against him, he boldly sang another verse, and one by one his would be slayers fell to earth overcome by the power of music(?).

Brother Mikell is evidently struck by Cupid's arrow, judging from the immense amount of bad poetry that he produces."

Cadet Peter Keys McCully is now the Corresponding Secretary. He began the above report with a reference to the ongoing battle with the "barbs" in which the Greeks were denied officer positions in the Polytechnic Society because of a "strong barbarian combination".

Nonetheless, at the upcoming Commencement exercises, Theta men will be well represented. Cadet William Howe Simons is the Valedictorian, first in his class of 37 men. Theta will also have more speakers at commencement than any other fraternity.

Theta men excelled militarily, with men winning compliments in the competitive drilling. Cadet Peter Keys McCully had previously won best drilled cadet in the entire Corps.

The disputed Cadet Picnic was held on May 2, 1890 and without the "barbarians" there, it became a big fraternity party. Fraternity colors were worn by the ladies with colors of the various fraternities being swapped about. To make matter worse, some cadets wore their fraternity colors on their gray uniforms. Even members of the Rho chapter at the University of South Carolina attended as well as "a large number of K.A. alumni". No doubt, the leadership at the Citadel took note of these infractions and set about to do something about them in the near future.

Volume VII, issue No.9, of *The Kappa Alpha Journal* published in June, 1890 contains the following report from Theta chapter.

"A certain sadness comes over the C.S. as he takes up his pen for the last time this year. Before this letter is published Theta will have received a hard blow, in the loss of seven as loyal knights as ever enlisted under the banner of the Crimson Cross. On commencement these men will for the last time add, as active members to Theta's laurels. Brother Simons, first graduate, is Valedictorian of the class. Brothers Dixon and Mikell are respectively Orator and Valedictorian of the Calliopean Literary Society, while Brothers Singletary and Greer fill the same position for the Cadet Polytechnic society.

Five men out of the seven to speak at commencement and all of then selected for the places which most require eloquence in speech and grace in delivery. The relative number of men in the different chapters here is as follows:

	KA	**ΣN**	**ΣAE**	**ATΩ**
Class of 1890	7	7	3	3
Class of 1891	5	1	2	1
Class of 1892	2	3	1	1
Class of 1893	3	3	3	2
Total	17	14	9	8
Return next year	10	7	6	5

There is one other organization here that calls itself a chapter of Pi Kappa Alpha, but it is not recognized by the Greek world, and is also a factor in the "barbarian" league", and therefore I can furnish no information about it, except that it is dragging on a sort of half-hearted existence.

On the competitive drill we were not as successful as we had hoped. We were not without honors, however, for Brother Mauldin won the prize from "B" company and it was the universal opinion that , but for manifest unfairness on the part of one of the judges Brother McCully would have won it in Company "D". Company "D" recently presented her Captain, Brother Dixon, with a very hand-

some sword and belt as a token of regard and recognition of the way in which he commanded the company on the competitive drill.

Brother Robertson is anxious to be a newspaperman, at least he is trying to get the position of cadet correspondent to the Charleston World.

Brother Singletary has been elected to respond to the toast "Class of 1890" at the banquet of the Association of Graduates of the South Carolina Military Academy.

In just the last debate between the two literary societies here, Brother Magrath represented the Calliopean and Brother Hart, the Polytechnic Society. Brother Hart, although just a "rat" is rapidly making for himself the reputation of being one of the best orators in the Academy.

Brother Zemp has been at his home in Camden for long while, down with typhoid fever; he is recovering now and soon we will have the pleasure of putting the grip on him once more.

There is some talk about having an encampment of the corps at some place in the northern part of the state, but nothing has been decided on yet."

The above entry in the *Journal* of June, 1890 is the last written report from a Corresponding Secretary for Theta Second chapter. It begins with a recitation of the honors achieved by the Theta men at the Commencement ceremonies. It adds the honors achieved in the drilling competition where Theta did well, but not as good as they expected.

The Corresponding Secretary provides a chart of the fraternity men in each of the 4 fraternities for the 1890-1893 classes. It appears that Kappa Alpha has the largest contingent.

Classes were over for the 1890 school year and after Commencement,

the cadets went their separate ways for the summer months. Kappa Alpha never received another formal report from Theta chapter. However, *The Kappa Alpha Journal,* volume VIII, number 3, published in December, 1890 did list a group of recent initiates of Theta and their dates of initiation as follows;

"Peter Keys McCully, Anderson, S.C., July 1, 1889

Francis Barron Grier, Gaithriesville, S.C., October 19, 1889

William Bicell Daniels, Augusta, GA., November 16, 1889

John Ratchford Hart, Yorkville, S.C., November 16, 1889

Charles Livingston O'Neal, Columbia, S.C., November 16, 1889

Robert McCaw Perrin, Abbeville, S.C., June 25, 1890

Robert Benjamin Gilchrist, Charleston, S.C., October 18, 1890"

It would appear from this list that Theta Second carried out at least one initiation after the beginning of the 1890 school year in October. So, in October, 1890, the chapter was still alive in spite of activities going on to ban it.

Unbeknownst to the Theta brothers, events were in motion by the summer of 1890 to enforce the prohibition on fraternities at The Citadel. The Board of Visitors met and directed that the following communication be read to the assembled Corps and a copy given to each cadet.

EXTRACT

FROM THE PROCEEDINGS OF THE BOARD OF VISITORS OF THE SOUTH CAROLINA MILITARY ACADEMY, JULY 1st, 1890.

Ordered, That the following communication be read upon Dress Parade, and that a printed copy be furnished to each Cadet before the close of the present session :

" It has come to the attention of the Board of Visitors that there exist in the Academy one or more secret societies, and as the existence of such societies is utterly incompatible with the purpose and organization of a Military Academy, and the Board has seen and felt the evil effects of the maintenance of these societies, therefore it is Ordered, that all Cadets who enter the Academy hereafter must, in addition to the Matriculation promise, subscribe to a promise not to join, or in anywise affiliate with, any secret society while they remain in the Academy.

"In the effort to suppress this vital evil, the Board calls to the attention of Cadets who may have joined such societies, that they have inadvertently violated their matriculation promise to obey the existing regulations of the Academy. Par. 192 provides, · That no society shall be organized among the Cadets without special license from the Superintendent.'

"These secret societies have neither sought nor obtained such permission. The Board calls upon such Cadets, in the interest of their Alma Mater and to the end that they may honorably discharge the obligations which they have assumed, to cease to affiliate with such societies during their Cadetship."

[signatures]

Courtesy: The Citadel Archives & Museum, Charleston, SC

As noted above, Theta chapter actually initiated one brother, Cadet Robert Benjamin Gilchrist, several months after the prohibition order was promulgated. However, the new directive and interpretation of Paragraph 192 made it very clear secret societies were banned. Now, in addition to the Matriculation promise, Cadets were required to sign

Theta Second Chapter: 1885 - 1890

a new oath not to join such societies while they were cadets.

The Board of Visitors met again in September, 1890 and reaffirmed the ban on secret societies.[1]

Finally capitulating to the inevitable, by a letter dated November 25, 1890, the Theta charter was sent back to the Grand Historian of Kappa Alpha Order, T.T. Hubard. This was confirmed in a letter from Cadet Magrath.

The Citadel cadets were not alone in facing the consequences of the anti-fraternity laws. On February 3, 1891, the Board of Visitors of the Virginia Military Institute met and despite pleas from various fraternity representatives, voted to keep in place regulations prohibiting

fraternity activity on campus.

As noted earlier, a state law was in effect from 1897 to 1927 prohibiting secret societies at state institutions. The Citadel prohibition remained in the College Regulations in substantially the same form becoming paragraph 186 in 1890, paragraph 185 in 1901, paragraph 155 in 1907, paragraph 96 in 1922, paragraph 80 in 1923 and 1926, paragraph 84 in 1929, paragraph 80 in 1934, paragraph 77 in 1948, and paragraph 76 in 1955.

The current prohibition is found in Section IV of the current college regulations.

"6. Clubs, Societies, and Associations. Requests for official recognition of clubs, societies, or associations on campus will be submitted through the sponsoring Citadel organization and the Director of Cadet Activities to the Commandant of Cadets or the Provost/Designee of the Provost, as appropriate, with details of organization, membership, purpose, and financing. For each society, association, or club formed by cadets or non-cadet students, and recognized officially by the College, there shall be an advisor who will be either a faculty or staff member selected by the association or appointed by the Commandant of Cadets or the Provost/Designee of the Provost, as appropriate, and who will confer with and advise the officers of such organization. All books and accounts of such organizations will be subject to inspection by the advisor and the Director of Cadet Activities or the Designee of the Provost, and no payments shall be made or debts contracted except on approval of the advisor. The Commandant of Cadets or the Provost/Designee of the Provost, as appropriate, shall publish regulations governing the administration of the funds of such organizations to include a requirement for periodic audits. The College assumes no liability for any indebtedness by such organizations, except those funded by the College. **Cadets will not belong to associations or fraternities of**

other colleges or universities without the prior approval of the President." (emphasis supplied).

So ended the early years of Theta Chapter. During this period, in spite of being *sub rosa*, the chapter had initiated some 43 men. They had built a functioning organization, successfully competed on campus with four other fraternities and created a lasting bond of brotherhood among their members. Their selection of brothers set a high standard for the future. Virtually every one of the 43 men initiated during this period led successful, productive lives. Doctors, lawyers, legislators, military officers, college presidents and professors were among their number. It can be said that these first men of Theta laid a solid foundation for the future.

Darkness now closed over Theta Chapter and for the next 30 years no fraternity activity would occur. There would be a brief flurry of initiations in the 1920-1924 timeframe, but those would be off campus and *sub rosa*. It would be some 118 years later, in 2008, before Theta would once again become active, this time as a Commission.

Endnotes

1. Board of Visitor Minutes, September, 1890.

Knights of the Order

XIV.
Theta Second Chapter, 1890-1920

*F*rom 1890 until 1920, Theta Second chapter was silent. As noted earlier, the name "Theta" was given to the State College (later University) of Kentucky in 1893. The Kentucky chapter operated as Theta and grew and prospered over the years.

During those 30 years from 1890 to 1920, individual members of Theta Second reported personal items of interest to The Kappa Alpha Journal. Marriages, births, deaths and promotions were all reported by loyal members of Theta Second even though their chapter did not exist. Among the reports were these;

The Kappa Alpha Journal, May, 1890

"William Edward Dick, a brother of three Dicks of Sigma (Davidson College) and charter member of Theta is farming at Sumter, S.C.

Thomas Perrin Harrison is now pursuing his studies at Johns Hopkins. His home is in Bradley, S.C.

George Yuille MacMurphy is studying medicine in Charleston, S.C.

Kenneth Gordon Matheson is Commandant of Cadets at the University of Tennessee, Knoxville, Tenn.

Beatie Andrew Inglis is a student at Stevens Institute, Hoboken. His home is Madison, Fla.

Council Black Ashley is practicing law in Madison, Fla.

Paul Hout Tamplet is cashier at the Bank of Georgetown, Georgetown, S.C.

Francis Ovid Spain is Assistant Professor of Mathematics, Georgia Institute of

Technology, Atlanta, Ga.”

The Kappa Alpha Journal, November, 1890

“William Edward Dick was married on November 12, 1890 to Annie Blanding of Sumter, S.C.”

The Kappa Alpha Journal, February, 1891

“Kenneth Gordon Matheson is commandant of Missouri Military Academy, Mexico, Missouri.”

The Kappa Alpha Journal, April, 1891

“George Yuille McMurphy is studying medicine in Charleston, S.C. His address is 50 Church St.”

The Kappa Alpha Journal, June, 1891

“Randolph Bradford Dunbar is farming near Beech Island, S.C.

Council Black Ashley is practicing law, Madison, Fla.

Evander McIver Law is a civil engineer, Brooklyn, N.Y.

George Morrall Gadsden is a civil engineer, Charleston, S.C.”

XV.
Theta Second Chapter 1920-1924

*I*n 1904, a Kappa Alpha chapter (Beta Gamma) had been established at the College of Charleston, located at the time only several blocks away from The Citadel. This chapter was established through the influence of The Rev. Henry J. Mikell, a brother of Alpha Alpha chapter at the University of the South, and a priest at the Church of the Holy Communion in Charleston. Mikell handpicked eight men to become the charter members of Beta Gamma. This was a small chapter as the college had less than 100 men and women students enrolled. We now know that 19 men from the Citadel were initiated into the Kappa Alpha Order by the Beta Gamma brothers between 1920 and 1924.

By this time, Kappa Alpha had begun assigning each initiate a badge number and formally recorded the date of the initiation. The 1920-1924 initiates were recorded by the Kappa Alpha Order National Administrative Office at the time as being in Theta Second Chapter. These men and the dates of their initiation are listed below.

May 6, 1920- Julius Blake Middleton

May 7, 1920- William Albert Dotterer, Hugh McCutchen James, Angus Wilson Riley, John Perryclear Scoville, Eugene Battle Smith, Lucian Cary Whitaker

October 23, 1920- Robert Edward Lee

June 11, 1920- Evander Ervin Brown, Louis Seel Poulnot

March 3, 1921- William Oscar Brice

March 4, 1921- John Lawrence Gramling, James Lee Platt

May 20, 1921- Thomas Quarles McGee

May 22, 1921- Benjamin Munnerlyn II, Orlando Clarendon Mood

April 19, 1922- Francis Banneau Carson

March 3, 1924- Eugene Williams Black

April 9, 1924- Marlborough Pegues

Further evidence of the initiations is found in the Beta Gamma reports filed with *The Kappa Alpha Journal* for that time period.

In *The Kappa Alpha Journal* Volume XXXVII number 4 of May, 1920, it reports there were three fraternities at the college: Kappa Alpha with ten members, Kappa Omicron with 13 members and Alpha Tau Omega with seven members. It also mentioned that Kappa Alpha had four "associate" members. It is believed that these four are some of the Citadel cadets recently inducted.

It should be noted that the fraternities at the College of Charleston during this time period were concerned about anti-fraternity rules. They were definitely aware of their questionable status in 1920. In The Kappa Alpha Journal report dated March, 1920, it was reported by the Beta Gamma chapter Corresponding Secretary, H.C. Harley that, *"the Chapter is discussing the bill which was before the Legislature for repealing the law forbidding fraternities in State Institutions. This is a very interesting subject and we all hope that the bill will go through."*(This is in reference to Act 322, passed in 1897). Nevertheless, apparently the college, as a private institution, tolerated the existence of fraternities in the early 1920's. The college yearbook for that period, *The Comet,* contains photographs and names of fraternity members of several fraternities.

Of more interest is just how did Citadel cadets in 1920 become so connected to Kappa Alpha members at the College of Charleston that they were invited to join. By that time, some 30 years had passed

Theta Second Chapter: 1920 - 1924

since the demise of Theta Second and the initiation of the last cadet in the fall of 1890. So, there would have been no institutional memory on the part of the 1920 cadets of Kappa Alpha or Theta Second or even a memory of fraternity activities. Instead, there were major impediments to a cadet joining a fraternity. Not only was it expressly forbidden in the matriculation promise each cadet signed, but for thirty years the prohibition had been rigidly enforced. Further, in 1897, Act 322 had become law making secret societies unlawful under state law. For a cadet to join a fraternity, thereby violating college regulations as well as state law was a blatant thing to do. Of the ten cadets initiated in 1920, four of them were seniors, initiated just a few months before graduation. If discovered, they risked being dismissed from school just days before their graduation. They were risking their entire college career by joining a fraternity at that point. What were the factors that led to this decision on their part?

For one thing, it might be the proximity of the two schools. Until 1922, the Citadel was located at Marion Square at the corner of King and Calhoun Streets. The College of Charleston was located at Calhoun and St. Philip Streets just two blocks away. Both were small schools, the Corps of Cadets being less than 200 men and the College of Charleston student body being less than 100. No doubt, when the cadets were permitted off campus, there was social contact between the two groups. Discussion ensued, friendships were formed and ideas exchanged, but what prompted the idea of that first initiation?

First, it should be noted that Beta Gamma would have been motivated to increase its membership by initiating cadets. Beta Gamma only had ten members in 1922 and that figure dropped to seven in 1923. So, for social reasons, having more Kappa Alpha brothers nearby, made for better parties, if for nothing else. Having social and financial motives to initiate Citadel cadets still did not answer the question of how did it come about?

The archives at the College of Charleston were searched in the hope that old fraternity records of the 1920 era may have been deposited there. The long time alumni advisor to Beta Gamma was interviewed regarding records. Nothing was uncovered. This was not unexpected, given the smallness of the college in 1920, as well as the fact that fraternities were outlawed by state law during that time period. (The College of Charleston was, at the time, a private school and State law may not have applied to them)

The author of this book was of the belief that family connections may also have played a critical part. It would make sense that a family with sons at both institutions at the same time could create the necessary mix to make this happen. First, there would have to be knowledge by a cadet of Kappa Alpha Order. Remember, that it had been thirty years since Kappa Alpha existed at The Citadel, well beyond the memory of a teenage cadet. Second, that knowledge would most likely come from a Kappa Alpha member at the College of Charleston, well-known to the cadet, who was motivated and could make the sale of joining a social fraternity. Finally, there needed to be a Kappa Alpha member of Beta Gamma with enough authority and initiative to motivate the chapter to not only initiate cadets, but get approval from the Knight Commander to do so.

This last ingredient was critical, since Kappa Alpha records indicated that the newly initiated cadets were not initiated and recorded as members of Beta Gamma, but were, in fact, recorded from the beginning as members of Theta (Second). That action indicated prior approval by Kappa Alpha Order and total support on their part of this initiative. This meant that while Kappa Alpha Order had accepted the charter surrender in 1890 and the chapter had been silent for thirty years, they still recognized Theta (Second).

Such a decision would have had to gain the approval of the Knight

Theta Second Chapter: 1920 - 1924

Commander at the time, H.C. Chiles. This decision would have been a bold one in view of the fact that the Theta charter and name from The Citadel had been given to the University of Kentucky in 1893.

With that background and logic, the author began looking for a family connection. Knowing the intricate family ties that exist in Charleston, the author set out to try and uncover the connection.

Initially, it was thought that the Beta Gamma connection and involvement began with a Charleston family by the name of Dotterer. On November 13, 1920, John Brinsdon Dotterer and Edwin Gaillard Dotterer, both students at the College of Charleston, were initiated into the Beta Gamma chapter. They were cousins residing in Charleston. They both later served as officers in Beta Gamma, John as the VI (Purser) and Edwin as the IV (Corresponding Secretary).

Their cousin, William Albert Dotterer, a junior cadet at the time, entered the Citadel in 1917 and was initiated by Beta Gamma on May 7, 1920. All of the connecting criteria were met except the fact that John and Edwin Dotterer did not become members of Kappa Alpha Order until <u>six months after</u> William was initiated. Given that fact, the case for the Dotterer family being the connection was weakened, if not eliminated.

The investigation continued with the author contacting various Kappa Alpha members who both knew Charleston family history and connections as well as Beta Gamma lore. Among those contacted was Douglas Bostick, a graduate of the College Of Charleston, '76, and a Beta Gamma initiate. Doug is also a full-time author/historian having written many books, mainly on the subject of the War for Southern Independence. Doug vaguely remembered some old documents that came into his possession in 1975.

As he tells it, "In 1974-1975, when we were working to re-charter Beta Gamma, I tried to track down every living Beta Gamma alumnus from the old chapter (1904-1936). Interestingly, there were many still alive. The widow of a chapter member from 1920 had the 1919-1920 Minute book and Chapter Registry in her husband's possessions and she was delighted to pass it along to someone seeking to revive what her husband had perpetuated."[1]

Brother Bostick had not only the Minute book, but the chapter registry from 1904-1936 that contained information on each member. He graciously shared the documents with this author and also sent a copy to Kappa Alpha Order National Administrative Office in Lexington, VA for safekeeping.

The minute records consist of 43 pages of hand written notes of numerous chapter meetings during the 1919-1920 school year. Most of the minutes are dated. Each of the minutes is signed by the chapter secretary.

The first set of minutes is undated, but was apparently from the first meeting of the school year in the fall of 1919 held on October 24th. These first minutes mention the initiation of Charles Frederick Poulnot, held that same night. It turns out that Charles Frederick Poulnot was not a new freshman student. He had in fact already spent two years (1917-1919) at The Citadel and had transferred to the College of Charleston as a junior. Records at The Citadel show that he was born on July 30, 1899 and attended Charleston High School. He entered The Citadel in the fall of 1917 as an 18 year old Pay cadet. At the end of the 1917-1918 school year he was ranked 45th of 121 members in his class in academic with only the first 66 making acceptable (passing) grades. Of the 260 members of the Corps, he was ranked 47 in conduct.[2]

Theta Second Chapter: 1920 - 1924

On September 12, 1918, at age 19, Charles went down and registered for the draft.

At the end of the 1918-1919 schoolyear, he was listed as "deficient" among his 74 classmates in academics. Only 33 of the 74 members of the sophomore class were found to be proficient in academics. This did not mean that Cadet Poulnot was not able to return to The Citadel his junior year. Unlike many of his classmates, he was not discharged for academic reasons, merely found to be deficient. Had he returned and made good grades his junior year, he would have been continued on the path to graduation. Instead, he chose to transfer to the College of Charleston, where he entered on September 28, 1919.

As mentioned earlier, Charles Poulnot was initiated by Beta Gamma chapter on October 24, 1919.

Going back to the chapter minutes, they indicate that chapter meetings were held on November 1st, 8th, 12th, 15th and 22nd. By the November 22nd meeting, Charles Poulnot was the acting Secretary and took minutes of the meeting as well as the meeting on December 6th. The regular Secretary, R. T. Jenkins, kept minutes of the December 10th, 13th, January 9th and January 17th meetings. It is interesting to note that at the January 17th meeting the chapter discussed lobbying the legislature to repeal the state law banning fraternities.

Another important thing happened at the January 17th meeting. The minutes reflected that "The Beta Amendment was also discussed by all members." This referred to the fact that in 1915, the Beta chapter at VMI, which had been suppressed for many years, had been converted to a Commission. (The Beta Amendment was the change to the Kappa Alpha Constitution that authorized the creation of a Commission. This change in the Constitution occurred at the 28th Convention of Kappa Alpha Order held at Richmond, VA on De-

cember 28th, 29th and 30th, 1915.)

Specifically, Section 168a was added to the constitution providing that: *"Any person who has attended the institution in which Beta Chapter of this Order was established for a period of two full years can be initiated into the Order under the following restrictions: Provided, First, the person possesses all the other qualifications necessary to become a member of this Order; Second, that the person shall be recommended to the initiating body by two members who are attending or who have attended the institution at which the said Beta chapter was established; Third, that the initiating body shall vote unanimously of its own free will to initiate such person; Fourth, that the K.C. shall give his written consent to the initiation of each individual thus initiated; Fifth, that the initiating body hereinabove mentioned shall consist of three alumni of Beta annually appointed by the Province commander of the Province in which Beta is or may be situated, shall have the power to adopt or reject the recommendation of any person as above provided, shall initiate or arrange for the initiation of such person and shall have in every case act(ed) with the counsel and cooperation of the Province Commander in which Beta is or may be situated."*

Charles Poulnot, probably due to his maturity and age, was clearly a leader in the group. At the January 19, 1920 meeting, he and another member tied for election to the Number II position of Vice-President. Charles was eventually appointed to this position which he held from January to June, 1920.

This meeting of January 19, 1920, was also the first mention in the chapter Minutes of initiating Citadel cadets. To quote from the minutes, "Bros. Palmer and Poulnot stated they had seen Bro. Brunnon regarding the Citadel Matter." Had the concept of initiating Citadel cadets been suggested by Charles Poulnot and was it being explored?

At the January 30, 1920 meeting, Charles Poulnot was appointed Number II. The Number I reported that the bill repealing the anti-

fraternity law had passed the state House of Representatives. No mention was made of the Citadel issue.

The February 7, 1920 chapter meeting contained the critical language regarding the Citadel. The minutes state that, "Bro. Poulnot was appointed by the G. M. to make a report on the history of the Order. Bro. Poulnot stated that he thought something should be done immediately to enable the chapter to take in men from the Citadel. Whereupon, it was moved and passed that the G.S.(Authors note: Secretary) be authorized to make application to the K.C. for the Beta Amendment." So, Charles Poulnot, a former cadet at The Citadel, now a Kappa Alpha member at the College of Charleston, leads his fraternity brothers in seeking to initiate cadets into a Commission similar to the one in existence at VMI.

The February 14th meeting passed without any reference to The Citadel, but the February 16th meeting minutes contained the following; "Bro. Hodges gave a summary of the whole Citadel matter and the Beta Amendment. After which several members gave their ideas on the situation.

The names of the suggested men were gone over in full and checked off, and it was decided that the committee, consisting of Bros. Owens of Rho chapter, Hill of Delta chapter and Jenkins of Beta Gamma chapter decide on the proposed men." This was indeed an important meeting. It began at 10:00pm and lasted until 1:15am the next morning. All chapter members were present along with brothers from both the University of South Carolina and Wofford College.

The chapter meeting of February 21st was held at the home of the Jenkins brothers. The minutes reflect that "Bro. Poulnot gave a very interesting history of the Order, which the President requested be put in the records of the chapter. The President gave an account

of the meeting of the committee to select men from The Citadel of which he was a member. He also read telegrams sent to the K.C.(Knight Commander) and Bro. Flinn, Province Commander of February 19th and letter sent the K.C.(Knight Commander) on the same date." Thus, we know that by February 19th, formal permission had been requested to initiate Citadel cadets into Kappa Alpha Order.

The meeting of February 28, 1920 contained another reference to the Citadel. The minutes state that the "President gave an account of the decision made by the Citadel committee. After which, the different brothers discussed the whole situation."

The meeting of March 5, 1920 again contained a reference to the Citadel matter. The minutes stated, "Bro. Palmer requested that two more names be added to the list of Citadel men to be taken in and also asked what requirements were necessary upon the passing of these men."

At the chapter meeting held on March 20, 1920, Charles Poulnot presided as the acting President. The meeting only lasted thirty minutes and nothing of consequence was done.

On March 27, 1920, Charles Poulnot again presided as acting Number I and the minutes reflected that "President asked Bro. Jenkins what further steps had been taken in the Citadel matter. Bro. Jenkins stated he would be forced to resign from the committee and that he had recommended Bro. Grissom to Bro. Flynn to fill his place on said committee. Bro. Jenkins also stated that he had advised Bro. Owens of his procedure". No explanation is given as to why Bro. Jenkins resigned.

The next chapter meeting was held on April 10, 1920 and again presided over by Charles Poulnot as acting President. The meeting lasted

one hour and fifteen minutes during which Bro. Biggart was initiated. Bro. Flynn, Commander of Smith Province was also present.

At the chapter meeting held on April 17, 1920, the elected President presided, but the Citadel matter was not mentioned. At the chapter meeting on April 24, 1920, the President reported "that seven of the Citadel men were put through the 1st degree on Friday night." This would mean that the first portion of the initiation had been performed for seven cadets.

The May 1, 1920 meeting of the chapter was uneventful. However, the May 15, 1920 minutes reflect the following entry: "Bro. Palmer reported that he was appointed by Bro. Owens to bid Mr. Lewis Poulnot of the Citadel, this action had already been taken with a favorable reply by Mr. Poulnot." Authors note: Lewis Poulnot was, in reality, Louis Seel Poulnot, a younger brother of Charles Poulnot. Louis Poulnot went on to graduate from The Citadel in 1922.

The May 20, 1920 chapter minutes reflect the following: "The chapter was called to order by the President at 4:15 pm. This was the first meeting held with the brothers taken in from The Citadel. Of those present were: Bros. Riley, Scovil(sp), Smith and Whitaker. The President welcomed the brothers into the chapter and read several important sections of the constitution." Authors note: Cadet Julius Blake Middleton was initiated on May 6, 1920. Cadets William Albert Dotterer, Eugene Battle Smith, Lucian Cary Whitaker, Angus Wilson Riley and John Perryclear Scoville were initiated on May 7, 1920.

The meeting of May 28, 1920 did not mention the Citadel situation; however the meeting of June 5, 1920 did refer to the cadets. The minutes reflected that, "There was a discussion by all brothers as to the taking in the Citadel men that had been pledged." No decisions were made.

Knights of the Order

The chapter meeting of June 10, 1920 was to be the final meeting of the school year. It was called to order at 3:00pm by the President. "President read the names of several men from The Citadel to be initiated on this coming Friday. Brother Smith said that three of the men mentioned would be unable to be initiated until the fall term." The chapter adjourned at 3:45pm. Authors note: Cadets Evander Ervin Brown and Louis Seel Poulnot were initiated on June 11, 1920. Cadet Robert Edward Lee was initiated on October 23, 1920, after the school year began in the fall, thereby completing the 1920 initiations.

In all during 1920, Beta Gamma initiated four Citadel seniors, just weeks before their graduation. They were Cadets Julius Blake Middleton, Hugh McCutchen James, Angus Wilson Riley and Eugene Battle Smith. They initiated three juniors during the same time period, Cadets William Albert Dotterer, John Perryclear Scoville, and Lucian Cary Whitaker. They also initiated three sophomores, Robert Edward Lee, Evander Ervin Brown and Louis Seel Poulnot. In total, during 1920, ten Citadel cadets were initiated by Beta Gamma brothers in four separate initiation ceremonies.

The accomplishment of having Beta Gamma chapter initiate Citadel men can be directly attributed to Charles Frederick Poulnot, the former Citadel student who transferred to the College of Charleston in the fall of 1919. He succeeded in raising the question, getting approval from Kappa Alpha Order and helped recruit the initiates, one of whom was his own brother. In a span of about six months, Charles Poulnot was initiated into Beta Gamma, elected the Number II, found out about the Beta Amendment, obtained permission from the Knight Commander and arranged the initiation of Citadel cadets, one of whom was his brother, Louis Seel Poulnot and four of whom were his former classmates at The Citadel, Cadets Brice, Platt, Scoville and Whitaker. This is quite an accomplishment.

Theta Second Chapter: 1920 - 1924

By May, 1921, the Beta Gamma practice of initiating cadets was out in the open. Their report to *The Kappa Alpha Journal* published in Volume XXXVII, number 3 announced,

"It gives the chapter great pleasure to introduce to the Order the following brothers, taken in on the 2nd of March, 1921;

> *John Lawrence Gramling*
>
> *William Oscar Brice*
>
> *Eugene William Black*
>
> *James Lee Platt."*

The report was signed by Edwin Gaillard Dotterer, Corresponding Secretary for Beta Gamma. Each of these four men were cadets at The Citadel. No mention is made of their Citadel connection, even though they were recorded by Kappa Alpha headquarters as members of Theta (Second).

Another connection to Beta Gamma may have been a unique uncle-nephew combination from two eras. In fraternity lore, "legacies" are family relationships in which the relative is given preference in admission to a fraternity organization. Benjamin A. Munnerlyn, Jr. was from Georgetown, S.C., and a cadet in the Class of 1886 (First Honor Graduate). Benjamin Munnerlyn, II, his nephew, born in Columbia, S.C. on September 16, 1901, was in The Citadel class of 1922. Benjamin Jr, was a Theta Second initiate (1884). Could it be that his nephew, learning of his uncle's positive fraternity experience in the 1880's, decided to follow in his footsteps and join his uncle's fraternity, Kappa Alpha Order. He would have been accepted almost automatically as a "legacy". Benjamin Munnerlyn, II, was initiated into Kappa Alpha on May 22, 1921. Could it be that Benjamin Mun-

nerlyn, II made contact with Beta Gamma, asking them to initiate him as a legacy?

Initiations by Beta Gamma continued until 1924. In 1921, six cadets were initiated. 1922 saw only one cadet initiated while in 1923, none were initiated. Finally, in 1924, two cadets were initiated, thus closing out the Beta Gamma involvement for the rest of the century.

Unlike the 1883-1890 era, there is no evidence that the men initiated in 1920-1924 ever held a chapter meeting or conducted normal fraternity activities. There is no evidence of fraternity activity on The Citadel campus. Perhaps, the men initiated attended Beta Gamma meetings or other activities even though there is no known proof of this. More than likely, each selection and initiation was highly secret with only friend to friend contact. Proof of this is found in the experience of the Howard family. Armstrong Jolly Howard, Sr. was a 1883 initiate. His son, Armstrong Jolly Howard, Jr. was a Citadel graduate of 1923, but not a Kappa Alpha initiate. It is highly likely that neither Howard knew of the existence of the Theta activities in the 1920's.

Items of personal interest concerning Theta members continued to appear in *The Kappa Alpha Journal.*

The Kappa Alpha Journal, October, 1919 listed Kappa Alpha service members in World War I. Under Theta Second are listed:

"Peter Keys McCully, Colonel, Infantry, Camp Sevier

William Howe Simons, Colonel, National Army, deceased"

The Kappa Alpha Journal, May, 1921

"Angus Wilson Riley married Margaret Evans on January 18, 1922 in Bennettsville, S.C. He is employed at the Union National Bank in Bennettsville."

Theta Second Chapter: 1920 - 1924

The Kappa Alpha Journal, November, 1922

"Peter Keys McCully moved from Anderson, S.C. to Greenville, S.C. having been made the selling agent of American Growers Association of S.C."

This issue also reported a number of deaths:

"Richard Wilson Riley, Barnwell, SC, September 30, 1922

Dr. William Ephriam Mikell, Dean of the Law Department, University of Pennsylvania

George Yuille MacMurphy"

The Kappa Alpha Journal, March, 1923

"Dr. Kenneth Gordon Matheson, and alumnus of The Citadel, The Military College of South Carolina, has recently been elected president of Drexel Institute at Philadelphia, at a salary of $16,500. Dr. Matheson has been president of Georgia Tech for about ten years and that institution was naturally very loath to give him up. He is a brother of Donald Stuart Matheson, Rho, a member of Kappa Alpha at the University of South Carolina and in 1895 transferred to Pi chapter and studied for some time at the University of Tennessee. Dr. Matheson has a son, K.G. Matheson, Jr, who became a member of Kappa Alpha at Georgia Tech last year."

The Kappa Alpha Journal, November, 1923

"Frank Barron Grier is President of the Charleston and Western Railroad with headquarters in Augusta, GA. He lives in Greenwood, S.C."

The Kappa Alpha Journal, May, 1924

"Reverend John Lake, Theta, Second, the Citadel and Mrs. Lake are spending a furlough in Edgefield, South Carolina after an absence of twenty years as missionaries in China."

Knights of the Order

The Kappa Alpha Journal, September, 1924

"Robert E. Lee, Theta, (Second), was graduated from the Citadel, the Military College of South Carolina, June 10th, 1924. His home is at Marion, South Carolina."

The Kappa Alpha Journal, January, 1925

"Benjamin Munnerlyn II, Theta (Second) and Miss Margaret Elizabeth Springs, daughter of the late Captain Albert Springs were married on November 19, 1924 in all Saints Church, Georgetown, S.C.

Paul Hout Tamplet, Theta (Second), former General Manager of Mutual Benefit Life Insurance Company of Newark, NJ died at his residence, the Ontario Apartments, Washington, D.C. on October 13, 1924. He was 50 years old, left a wife and two children. He is buried in Georgetown, S.C.

(Authors note: Tamplet was one of the original Founding Members of Theta Second Chapter)

James Lee Platt, Jr. Theta, (Second), has recently been admitted to the bar in South Carolina. He was graduated from the Citadel in 1920 and immediately matriculated in the law department of George Washington University, remaining there three years. He affiliated with Alpha Nu Chapter. He is well prepared and will no doubt rise steadily in the practice of his profession. "Judge Platt", we hope someday to be able to address him."

The Kappa Alpha Journal, January, 1926

"Hugh McCutchen James, Theta, (Second), and Miss Clara Pillott Tillman were married 28 December, 1925 in St. James Episcopal Church, Quitman, Georgia, the home of the bride. Mrs. James received her education at Goucher College and at the King Studio of Violin and Piano. The groom is a native of Summerton, South Carolina, but after his graduation from the Citadel in 1921, he taught

school at Quitman until the summer of 1925 when he returned to South Caro-
lina, locating at Columbia, where he is owner and manager of the James Battery
Service. He is a nephew of the late Hugh McCutchen, one of the first members
of Sigma Chapter, at Davidson College and of James Gilland McCutchen of
Rho Chapter."

"James Lee Platt, Jr, Theta, (Second), and Alpha Nu and Miss Rose Killan of
1733 First Street, Washington, D.C. were married 30 December, 1925, at the
home of the bride, the ceremony being performed by the Reverend Dr. J.J. Muir.
The groom is a graduate of the Citadel, Class of 1921. After his graduation
at the Citadel, he entered George Washington University for the study of law,
finishing the course with the degree of LL.B. in 1924. For two years during his
stay at George Washington he was business manager of "The Cherry Tree", the
university magazine. Returning to South Carolina, he was admitted to the bar
and opened offices for the practice of his profession at McColl, in the center of the
finest agricultural section of the South."

Theta (Second) Chapter Sequel

Kappa Alpha Order has made an effort to record the military service
of its initiates in all wars since the founding of the fraternity in 1865.
Accordingly, in a book entitled Kappa Alpha Military and Naval Record, 1865-1922 edited and typed in 1938 by W. S. Hamilton, Archivist, are recorded the following.

"Theta Second Chapter, South Carolina Military Academy, Charleston, S.C.

William Albert Dotterer, Jr. Candidate, M.G. O.T.S. Cp. Hancock

Thomas Perrin Harrison, Secretary, Y.M.C.A., Army Educational Corps, A.E.F.

Peter Keys McCully, Colonel, 118th Inf., 30th division, A.E.F., In all actions participated in by the 30th Division

Kenneth Gordon Matheson, Director of Division, Y.M.C.A., A.E.F., Soissons, near Verdun, Toul and along the Marne.

William Howe Simons, Captain, 6th U.S. Vol. Inf. Philippines. Colonel, 164th Inf. 82nd Division. Died in service, 4-13-18

Robert McCaw Perrin, Adjutant with rank of Captain, Cp. Beauregard"

Meanwhile, it is appropriate to follow to its conclusion the life of the man who resurrected Theta Chapter, if only briefly. Charles F. Poulnot left the College of Charleston when the school year ended in 1920. Even though he had completed three years of college work, he did not graduate. He married Edith Oliver and was employed during most of his life as manager of Kerrison's Department Store in Charleston, a family enterprise. Charles died on November 26, 1971 and his wife, Edith died in 1991. Both are buried at Magnolia Cemetery in Charleston, S.C. Theta owes a huge debt to the initiative and courage of Charles Frederick Poulnot. Without his leadership, the 19 men initiated in the 1920's would not be members of the Order.

With these publications, the era of Theta Chapter at The Citadel came to an end. A total of 62 men had been initiated. A reading of their biographies later in his book shows that for the most part they were outstanding citizens and leaders in their communities. Among

them were a world renowned Missionary, a college President, a law school Dean, several medical doctors, two state legislators, one of whom became a Circuit Judge, several bankers, college Professors, numerous attorneys, a four star General, a two star General, numerous Colonels, businessmen and farmers. Four of them (William O. Brice, John Lake, Thomas P. Harrison and Frank Barron Grier) had the distinction of being awarded Honorary Degrees from their Alma Mater in later years. The Citadel did not begin awarding Honorary Degrees until 1929 and had they done so earlier there is no question, but that William Howe Simons, William E. Mikell and perhaps others of this era would have received one. Simons is extolled in effusive terms in President Bond's book and was given a sword by the Board of Visitors on his departure as Commandant in 1908. Mikell was the featured speaker at the 1908 Commencement. Five of them, (William Howe Simons, Armstrong Jolly Howard, Frank Barron Grier, Thomas Joab Mauldin and Robert McCaw Perrin) have windows in Summerall Chapel dedicated in their memory. These 62 men were indeed a noteworthy group, whose achievements set a high bar for the future.

They had forged a solid foundation, but it would be up to a future generation of Citadel men to carry the Theta name forward in another century. That interesting story begins in the 1950's.

Endnotes

1. Interview with Douglas Bostick, July, 2013.

2. Annual Report to the General Assembly, 1917-1918, 1918-1919.

Knights of the Order

XVI.
THE BIRTH OF THETA COMMISSION
2008-PRESENT

THE CAPED CRUSADER

*W*ith the initiation of Cadet Marborough (Mollie) Pegues in 1924, further cooperation between Beta Gamma and Theta Second ended and Kappa Alpha Order ceased to exist at the Citadel when Cadet Pegues graduated in 1924. For the next 84 years, until 2008, Theta was silent.

In writing a history of Theta's renewal, it is tempting to identify one individual and label him as the "Father of Theta Commission", similar to Philip Hamer being the "Father of Theta Chapter". However, research has revealed that like most great accomplishments, many individuals were involved at various critical moments. There was no one "Father". That Theta was resurrected at all is a complex story. And while many men were later involved, we can say that one colorful, talented and dedicated man was there at the very beginning. Without his involvement, there would likely be no Theta Commission today. Here is that story.

In June of 1996, at a small, private, all-male boarding school in the northwestern section of Virginia, two men in sweat clothes and running shoes found themselves running side by side in a 5 kilometer race. One of those men was Gordon Saussy Varnedoe, whose nickname, acquired in the 1960's was "Bat", which later morphed into

"Batman". Batman was born in 1938, while the comic book character made famous by DC Comics was first published in 1939. Hence, his wife suggests that all the Batmen who followed, including those in the popular movies, were imposters and copycats.

Batman had been born in Savannah, Georgia to a prominent family. His father and older brother had gone to Woodberry Forest School in Virginia. So, it was natural for him to be sent there for high school in the fall of 1952. From the start, Batman and Woodberry Forest did not get along.

Set in a picturesque section of Virginia on 1,200 acres, the school with a student body of only 250 boys had tough rules. For instance, listening to music was forbidden. Batman loved all the popular music of the 50's, Elvis Presley, Fats Domino and Little Richard, among others. Nashville radio station WLAC broadcast non-stop rock and roll music and listening was a temptation Batman could not resist. Batman also loved girls and being locked in a boy's school in the country four miles from the small town of Orange, Virginia was not conducive to a good social life. The few social contacts with members of the opposite sex were heavily chaperoned.

On campus, there were stories of a young man, dressed in black, who roamed the campus at night visiting the attractive daughter of a local professor. Hence, the young man acquired the nickname of "Batman."

Studying was rigorous at Woodberry Forest, with mandatory study halls each evening presided over by a gruff faculty member. Wearing a coat and black tie to school every day also did not sit well with young Varnedoe. The school was simply not a friendly place for a rambunctious, fun loving, young man.

Nevertheless, Batman toughed it out and graduated in 1956 after having had five radios confiscated from his room over the four years. When he left in 1956 with a diploma in hand, he thought he had been given a parole from prison. He vowed never to return. After graduating in 1956, he put the school behind him and over the years ignored their solicitations for funds as well as reunion invitations.

He entered Emory University in Atlanta, Georgia in the fall of 1956 where he pledged the Epsilon Chapter, Kappa Alpha Order and was initiated in 1957. In 1958, he transferred to the University of Georgia and lived the full fraternity life in a Gamma chapter house there. In 1960, he was elected the Number I at Gamma chapter. He graduated from there in 1961, moved out west and went into sportswear sales.

Over the years, Batman was active in various Kappa Alpha Order activities. He was voted Alumnus of the Year at Gamma chapter and twice voted Alumnus of the Year at Delta Theta, as well as alumnus advisor. He was appointed Province Commander of Hardeman Province, consisting of nine chapters in the state of Georgia. He served as President of the Coastal Empire alumni chapter in Savannah, Georgia and was inducted into the Hardeman Province Court of Honor. Finally, he received the high honor of the Knight Commander's Accolade from Knight Commander David M. Warren in 2003 for excellence in leadership and service to the Order.

Varnedoe found time over the years for other activities. Possessing Scottish heritage, he entered the Scottish Highland Games in North Carolina in 1978 and won the first prize in Caber Tossing. The Caber is a large wooden pole, 19 feet six inches long and weighing 175 lbs. The idea is to toss it in the air by one end making a complete 180 degree rotation and landing exactly at the 12 o'clock position. Tossing Cabers gives one a clue to the fitness and athletic ability of this man. He also won 20 gold Medals in Masters Weightlifting and held the

American record for four years. He also claims the title of the oldest rugby player in Georgia and holds three world records in Powerlifting. These and other feats led to him being inducted into the Greater Savannah Athletic Hall of Fame in 2013.

By 1996, the bad memories of the 1950's at Woodberry Forest had faded and since he had many good friends who graduated with him, he decided to attend his 40th Reunion at the school. One of the events that weekend was a five kilometer run. He soon found himself at the back of the pack running next to a man he did not know. They struck up a conversation and soon, the man who hated the school in the 1950's, found that he was running next to the school's Headmaster, Major General John Grinalds.

General John Grinalds was born in Maryland, but spent most of his childhood in Macon, Georgia. He excelled in high school and entered West Point where graduated with honors in 1959. He became a Rhodes Scholar, graduating again with honors. After several assignments, he served two tours in Vietnam, being decorated there with the Silver Star for heroism. After Vietnam, he held numerous staff and command assignments. He earned his MBA from Harvard Business School and was a White House Fellow. He was promoted to Major General in 1989 and commanded the Marine Recruit Depot in San Diego before he retired in 1991.

Major General John S. Grinalds

In 1991, General Grinalds became the seventh Headmaster at Woodberry Forest School. While there, he was a very popular Headmaster who developed high standards, increased fundraising and modernized the school.

After their run, General Grinalds invited Varnedoe to the "Residence", the campus home of the Headmaster. There Varnedoe met Grinalds' wife, Norwood, and a friendship developed between the Grinalds and the Varnedoes. Varnedoe visited Woodberry Forest over the next two years and stayed at the "Residence". Grinalds convinced Varnedoe that the Woodberry Forest of the 1950's was no more. Now students walked around campus with ear buds and Sony Walkmans, listening to whatever they wanted to. There were also frequent mixers with girl's schools. In spite of the changes, Woodberry Forest was still an excellent school known for its academics.

Grinalds moved to The Citadel in August of 1997 as President and Varnedoe and his wife attended the inauguration as Grinalds' guests. Later, President George W. Bush visited the Citadel campus on December 11, 2001. Varnedoe was also invited to that event. In a visit to Grinalds office on December 12, 2001, after the Bush festivities, Varnedoe commented on a large portrait of Robert E. Lee hanging on the wall. General Grinalds wife, Norwood, had given him the portrait when he graduated from West Point many years before. Both men greatly admired Lee and Varnedoe mentioned Lee's connection to Kappa Alpha Order which Grinalds knew about. Varnedoe then asked Grinalds if he had any interest in joining Kappa Alpha Order. This invitation drew an enthusiastic, positive response from Grinalds who said that Kappa Alpha was the only fraternity he would ever consider joining because of Kappa Alpha's relationship to Robert E. Lee.

Becoming a "special initiate' of a Kappa Alpha chapter requires a letter of recommendation from a Kappa Alpha alumnus, the advisor

to the chapter, the Province Commander and a vote of the Executive Council and of the chapter. Varnedoe also asked Pat Conroy, the famous novelist and Citadel graduate, who knew General Grinald's well, to write a letter as a non-member.

In May 13, 2002, General John Grinalds was inducted into Delta Theta chapter of Kappa Alpha Order at Georgia Southern University.

At the time of Grinalds initiation, Varnedoe had no knowledge of the old Theta Second chapter of the 1880's at The Citadel, nor any thoughts of a Commission of Kappa Alpha there. The two men were simply friends, sharing a Georgia background (Macon and Savannah), a boarding school connection (Woodberry Forest), and a deep respect for the values embodied in Robert E. Lee and southern traditions.

Some months later, Knight Commander David M. Warren asked Executive Director Larry Wiese to find out if Batman would help them with an introduction to Grinalds to explore the possibility of a Commission of Kappa Alpha Order at The Citadel. Batman agreed and a meeting, followed by a lovely luncheon at the President's House on the Citadel campus, hosted by Norwood Grinalds, was held on Monday, the 16th of September, 2002.

The Birth of Theta Commission 2008 - Present

L to R, "Batman Varnedoe", Executive Director Larry Wiese, future Knight Commander, Ben W. Satcher, Jr, General John Grinalds, Knight Commander David M. Warren, Pres. Coastal GA, alumni chapter, Allen Vance, future Knight Commander Mike Duncan, Executive Council member, Russell Brown. Photo courtesy of J. Michael Duncan.

The entire group of Kappa Alpha Order senior officers was present, to include Knight Commander David Warren, future Knight Commanders Ben W. Satcher, Jr. and J. Michael Duncan and Executive Director Larry Wiese. At the luncheon, Norwood Grinalds proudly showed a photo of herself attending an Old South Ball. No further action was taken on the Commission concept by Kappa Alpha Order until 2007. This decision was based on the belief by General Grinalds that the time was just not right for such a move. Despite a desire to develop a Commission at The Citadel, all efforts to create one were put on hold.

General Grinalds later said this about his decision to join Kappa Alpha Order.

Knights of the Order

"As you know, Gordon "Batman" Varnedoe invited and encouraged me to become a member of Kappa Alpha Order, and arranged for my induction and initiation into the Delta Theta Chapter at Georgia Southern University. That occurred on May 13, 2002.

The influence of the examples of Gordon and several of my childhood friends, who became members of KAO in college, all men of high character, was significant in my desire to become a member as well. However, of greatest importance were the values of Kappa Alpha Order, in particular that of reverence. Being in the company of men who acknowledge and practice a deep reverence for God is eloquent testimony to His sovereignty and saving grace in our lives. I wanted to be part of that testimony in forming the values of our nation's future leaders."

Robert B. Varnado, Gordon S. (Batman)Varnedoe and Major General John S. Grinalds at a Theta Commission meeting on March 6, 2013. Authors collection.

THE CHARLESTON THREE

Robert (Rob) Bratton Varnado was born in, Hartford, CT. to parents, both of whom were from Texas. He graduated from East Cooper High School in Mt. Pleasant, S.C. in 1987. After high school he attended the University of the South in Sewanee, Tennessee, receiving his B.A. degree in 1990. Thereafter, he attended the University of South Carolina Law School in Columbia, S. C., graduating in 1994. After taking and passing the bar exam, he began practicing law in Charleston, S.C.

While at college, Varnado joined the Kappa Alpha (Alpha Alpha) chapter at Sewanee. He was active in fraternity activities holding the office of III and IX. After he began his law practice he continued his interest in Kappa Alpha by attending the Kappa Alpha conventions in Tampa and Savannah. He was also the local alumni advisor to Beta Gamma chapter at the College of Charleston.

In the Kappa Alpha organizational hierarchy, chapters in one area are grouped into "provinces" for administrative purposes. Thus, all Kappa Alpha chapters in South Carolina are grouped under what is known as Graves Province. This province is named for John Temple Graves, a former Knight Commander (1881) from South Carolina and noted southern journalist.

In the fall of 2007, Knight Commander J. Michael Duncan called Brother Robert Varnado and asked him to fly to St. Louis, MO. The stated purpose was for Varnado to be interviewed as one of two applicants for the post of Commander of Graves Province. Varnado argued that he was not the right person for the position for the simple reason that he had not been initiated into Kappa Alpha Order from a school within the Province, the University of the South being in Tennessee. Varnado urged the Knight Commander to select

G. Randall (Randy) Smith, a highly qualified individual who met those qualifications and who resided in Greenville, S.C. The Knight Commander would not be deterred and insisted that Varnado meet him in St. Louis which Varnado did in November, 2007.

Unknown to Varnado, the Knight Commander had another mission in mind. Upon arriving at the meeting, the Knight Commander informed Varnado that on reflection, he had decided to accept Varnado's advice and appoint the other man for the post. Varnado was ultimately appointed Graves Deputy Province Commander for Academic Affairs in 2008. Knight Commander Duncan and Executive Director Larry Wiese, who was also present, then asked Varnado if he would lead an effort to establish a Kappa Alpha Commission at The Citadel.

The idea for a Commission at The Citadel was not a new idea. At a meeting of the Kappa Alpha Order Executive Council on March 14-16, 2002, then Knight Commander David M. Warren appointed a committee to explore establishing commissions at the Air Force Academy, West Point and The Citadel. On that committee were J. Michael Duncan and Russell Brown. Further discussions took place at the Executive Council meetings of August 7-10, 2002 and August 3-7, 2004. While the Order desired to establish these Commissions, for various reasons no progress was made. At the August 3-7, 2004 meeting, Councilor Brown moved that the idea be tabled for the time being and this motion passed unanimously. The matter of Commissions was dormant until the fall of 2007.

Through his work on the earlier committee in 2002, Knight Commander Duncan was already a strong proponent of a Commission at The Citadel. In fact, he wanted to create Commissions at The Citadel as well as at all the service academies. The question became one of how to get the proverbial foot in the door. Duncan felt that going in and directly recruiting active cadet members was not appropriate. He

The Birth of Theta Commission 2008 - Present

felt that establishing a Commission composed of older alumni members first was the best approach and this is what he and Larry Wiese proposed to Brother Varnado.

Varnado, along with two of his friends, all Kappa Alpha brothers, were aware of the desire for a Kappa Alpha Commission at The Citadel. The three men had discussed among themselves the possible opportunity for Kappa Alpha to take a different approach in building a Commission at The Citadel. Varnado agreed with the Knight Commander that if a Commission composed of older alumni were established first, it just might work. Once established, the Commission could add younger, recent graduates at a later date.

Knight Commander Duncan, in appropriate fashion, put Varnado and his two Kappa Alpha brothers in Charleston in charge of implementing this plan, which was very similar to the existing Commission at the Virginia Military Institute.

The Beta Chapter of Kappa Alpha Order was established at Virginia Military Institute on March 8, 1868. This was a natural expansion, since VMI was located adjacent to Washington College where Kappa Alpha originated in 1865. With the advent of the anti-fraternity laws, the Beta Chapter was suppressed over the years. VMI had similar cadet regulations to those at The Citadel which prohibited fraternity membership.

Finally, it was converted to a "Commission" in 1915. As a commission, it functions by only initiating men into Kappa Alpha after their graduation. At the Virginia Military Institute, the "Commission" is composed of five men, usually VMI professors, who nominate selected senior cadets and alumni for initiation into Kappa Alpha each year. The initiation ceremony is usually performed immediately after

the cadet completes his Commencement Day services and receives his diploma from VMI. In 2013, the initiation ceremony was moved to the week prior to graduation.

Upon his return to South Carolina, Varnado called upon his two friends to assist him. The group would become known later in Theta Commission circles as the "Charleston Three". The other two were A. Donald Evans of Cheraw, S.C. and Baron Fain of Dallas, TX., both of whom were now living in Charleston.

Evans had attended the Citadel in 1977-1978, withdrawing after one year because of his father's illness. Evans later completed his education at Francis Marion University where he pledged Kappa Alpha Order, joining the Delta Tau chapter. Evans was, by late 2007, in the real estate investment business in Charleston and active in a number of civic organizations. He was a prominent member of the Charleston business community. He also had many friends who were Citadel graduates.

Earl Fain IV, known as "Baron", was born in New York, raised in Dallas, TX. and had relatives in South Carolina. He attended the University of the South, where he joined Alpha Alpha chapter of Kappa Alpha Order in 1982. After graduating in 1985, he worked on Capitol Hill for four years before enrolling in graduate studies at the University of Virginia. He received a Masters in Foreign Affairs in 1992 from the University of Virginia. He moved to Charleston in 1992, where he is the institutional sales manager for an international retailer.

Fain was active in numerous civic and social organizations both in Charleston and across the country. These included the Order of St. John, Freemasons, Odd Fellows, Military Order of the Stars and Bars, St. David's Society, Sons of Confederate Veterans, Sons of the American Revolution, Palmetto Guard, the Washington Light Infantry, the Society of Colonial Wars and others. He was also active in St.

Philip's Church in Charleston.

These three men shared numerous traits and interests. To begin
with, they were all men of faith, and all were members of St. Philip's
Church. In fact, they saw each other frequently in church- related activities. All three were also true patriots, who had an abiding love for
America. While they shared the Kappa Alpha connection, all three
were also in other organizations together such as the Palmetto Guard,
the Carolina Yacht Club and St. David's Society. Evans and Fain were
in the Sons of Confederate Veterans together. All three were also
members of the Magnolia Masonic Lodge in Washington, DC, whose
members were all Kappa Alpha brothers.

Another remarkable connection was their collective love of history,
particularly southern history. Both Varnado and Fain had majored in
history in college while Evans missed getting his major in history by
only 6 hours of course work. All three had a genuine love for the Old
South with its family ties and patriotic traditions.

The three of them met for lunch on November 6, 2007, where they
fleshed out their plan. They needed at least five men to constitute the
first class of initiates, so they talked among themselves about who
they knew and who would approach whom. It became immediately
clear that Evans, because of his Citadel and business connections
would be the most effective in approaching potential members.

However, it turned out that each of the three knew and easily agreed
upon all five men ultimately selected. Varnado knew Brandt through
the St. David's Society and the French Society, he knew Rembert as
a family friend and at the Carolina Yacht Club, he knew Crawford
through the Palmetto Guard, he knew Tant through a Masonic Lodge
connection, he knew Harrington through the Episcopal Church.
Fain knew Rembert through St. Philips Church, the Carolina Yacht

Club and the Sons of Confederate Veterans. He knew Tant from Masonic work, he knew Harrington through both the church and the Washington Light Infantry. He knew Crawford through Sons of Confederate Veterans, St. David's Society, St. Philips Church, the Palmetto Guard, and the Carolina Yacht club.

Varnado, Evans and Fain were not looking for just any five men. They wanted leaders, respected in their professions and in their community. They wanted men of deep religious conviction. They wanted men whose names alone would give instant credibility to Kappa Alpha Order within the Citadel community. They also wanted leaders upon whom an organization could be built.

Various names were mentioned, some were accepted and some rejected. They wanted only the best. Six men were initially selected, but one dropped out for personal reasons. They finally settled on five men, who they believed should be the founding members of Theta Commission.

History would judge their choices to be truly outstanding. They were:

Colonel James A. W. Rembert, Class of 1961. Colonel Rembert served in Company "T" while a cadet. Rembert was a leader while at the Citadel serving as a Chairman of the Honor Committee and Cadet Major his senior year. Upon graduation, he entered the United States Army, completing Infantry School, Airborne and Ranger Schools before joining the 11th Special Forces Group (Airborne). After his military service, he obtained

James A. W. Rembert

his MA degree in English at the University of South Carolina and his Ph.D in English at the University of North Carolina at Chapel Hill

and a second Ph.D in English at Cambridge University in England. He taught English at the Citadel for 41 years. While a professor, he taught abroad at Jesus College, Cambridge University and was a Fulbright Lecturer at Guangdong University of Foreign Studies in Canton, China. He also served as a consultant for the American Battle Monuments Commission and the Medal of Honor Museum. He was Associate Editor and Military Affairs Editor for the Charleston *Mercury* newspaper. Upon his retirement, he was awarded the Palmetto Medal, the second highest award given by the Board of Visitors. He is married to Celia Childress Rembert and they have 5 children.

Colonel Myron C. Harrington, Jr.

Class of 1960. Harrington was in Company "F" while a cadet. He received a B.A. degree in History. Upon graduation, he entered the United States Marine Corps completed Basic School and was commissioned a Second Lieutenant. He commanded Delta Company, 1st Battalion, 5th Marines during the fierce battle for Hue, South Vietnam in

Myron C. Harrington, Jr.

1968. For his conspicuous bravery leading his men, he was awarded the Navy Cross, second only to the Medal of Honor in recognizing valor in armed combat. He was also awarded the Silver Star, Legion of Merit with two Gold Stars, Meritorious Service Medal with one Gold Star, Navy Commendation Medal with Combat V with Gold Star, Vietnamese Cross of Gallantry, with Gold Star and the Vietnamese Staff Honor Medal, First Class. Harrington spent a 31 year career in the USMC rising to the rank of full Colonel and received numerous other service awards. His final assignment was Professor of Naval Science and Commanding Officer of NROTC at The Citadel. He spent a second career from 1992- 2007, as Headmaster

Knights of the Order

at Trident Academy. He was Co-Chair of the 2010 Medal of Honor Convention, Vice-Chair of the Mt. Pleasant War Memorial Committee, Senior Warden, St. Philip's Church, Past President of the Charleston Foreign Affairs Forum, Past President of the Charleston Chapter of the Navy League, and Secretary to the Board of Visitors. Colonel Harrington is also a member of the Rotary Club, The Society of Colonial Wars, Sons of Confederate Veterans, Washington Light Infantry, Order of St. John and the Clergy Society. He received the Order of the Palmetto, the highest award given by the State of South Carolina. He married Ann Randolph Hurst in 1965 and they have two children.

Brigadier General Hugh Banks Tant, III

Hugh Banks Tant, III

Class of 1971. General Tant served in Company "E" while a cadet. He received his B.S. in Business Administration and was a Distinguished Military Graduate. He was also a Gold Star student and a member of the Economic Honor Society. Tant entered the United States Army and served for a total of just over 30 years. During that time, he received his MA in Business Management, graduated from the Command and General Staff College (Honor Graduate), the Armed Forces Staff College and the U.S. Army War College. He rose from Second Lieutenant to Brigadier General. General Tant was awarded the Distinguished Service Medal, The Legion of Merit, The Bronze Star, The Defense Meritorious Service Medal, The Meritorious Service Medal (3 awards), The Army Commendation Medal (3 awards), the Expert Infantryman's Badge, The Master Parachutist Badge, The Air Assault Badge, Southwest Asia Service Medal, the Saudia Arabian Kuwait Liberation medal, and the Overseas Service ribbon. General Tant was tasked by Ambassador Paul

Bremer to manage the Iraqi currency exchange in 2003 in an effort to jumpstart the Iraqi economy. This task was accomplished in six months, under fire. He received the U.S. Treasury Department's highest award, the Distinguished Service Award. In retirement, Tant was active in numerous civic organizations and went back to college to become fluent in German. He was a Senior Vice President at Southcoast Community Bank from 2003-2008. He was also Executive Director of Patriot's Point Development Authority from 2008-2009. He is married to Christine Lee Tant and they have twin daughters, Anna and Elizabeth.

Julian Victor Brandt, III, Class of 1972. Mr. Brandt served in Company "A" while a cadet. He received a BA in History. After college, he received his real estate license and entered his family real estate firm in Charleston, specializing in historic properties. He is a graduate of the Realtors Institute. Over the years, he has been active in historic preservation

Julian Victor Brandt, III

and a recognized leader in that area in his community. Brandt personally worked on restoring over 30 historic buildings. He was appointed by the Mayor to serve on the Board of Architectural Review from 1978-1986 and was its Chair. He was a member and officer of the Preservation Society, The Old Exchange Building Commission and the College Preparatory School. He has authored articles for trade magazines on real estate subjects and lectured on historic preservations subjects. He authored articles published in both the Charleston Magazine and the Charleston *Mercury*. Brandt was active in numerous civic clubs, including the Washington Light Infantry, the Charlestowne Neighborhood Association, the Footlight Players, La Societe Francaise, Sons of the American Revolution, Sons of Confederate

Veterans, Society of the War of 1812, St. David's Society, Society of King Charles, the Martyr, Royal Society of St. George, The Huguenot Society, The Hibernian Society, St. George's Society of New York, the Military Order of the Stars and Bars, The Napoleonic Society and the English Speaking Union. He was also a member of the Order of St. John. He is an active member of St. Michael's Church. Brandt married Anne Read and they have 3 children.

Alexander (Lex) S. Crawford, Class of 1977. Mr. Crawford served in Company "L" while a cadet. While at the Citadel, Crawford was a member of the Calliopean Literary Society and the Salute Gun Battery. Upon graduation, he received a BS in Business Administration degree. He went to work from 1978-1983with Port Oil Company in Mobile, Alabama and rose to the position of President. He later joined the Charleston Harbor

Alexander S. Crawford

Pilots Association and spent 15 years there where he was a Senior Boat Captain. He was currently employed by the SC Department of Transportation. Crawford was active in various civic endeavors. He is a member of the Sons of Confederate Veterans, Palmetto Guard (Commander, 2005-2006), South Carolina Historical Society, St. David's Society, and the Sumter Guard. He served as both a member, officer and on the Board of the Edisto Island Open Land Trust. He is a member of St. Philip's Protestant Episcopal Church. He married Anne Hendricks and they have 4 children.

Evans contacted Rembert, Harrington, Tant and Crawford, while Varnado contacted Brandt. All accepted the invitation to join the Kappa Alpha Order. Varnado actually performed background checks on each man.

However, it was not quite as simple to establish Theta Commission as everyone initially thought. There was no Theta Commission in existence. After consulting the Kappa Alpha Constitution and Bylaws, it was determined that the five selected men must first be inducted into a Kappa Alpha chapter, then apply themselves, for a Commission Charter. Once again, as it had done in the 1920's era, Beta Gamma chapter at the College of Charleston played a major role in Theta history.

Men selected for special initiation in Kappa Alpha Order must pass a selection process by the Executive Council and be approved for initiation by a unanimous vote of the initiating chapter. That meant getting the approximately 35 current members of Beta Gamma chapter to unanimously approve of all five of these men, none of whom they had ever met. One "no" vote by a member of Beta Gamma and the best laid plans of the Knight Commander and the "Charleston Three" would be shot down.

Varnado was given the task of obtaining the unanimous consent from Beta Gamma. This occurred at a meeting with the chapter on March 10, 2008. The Beta Gamma meeting was held in a classroom of the Albert Simons Performing Arts Center. He describes the trepidation he felt making the presentation to the crowded room of 35 Beta Gamma's. At the end of his presentation, he left the room while they discussed and voted on his request. He waited outside the room like an expectant father in the maternity section of a hospital waiting to hear whether Theta Commission would be born or not. Varnado describes the meeting as follows;

"At the time it voted on the applications of founders, Beta Gamma held its chapter meetings on Sunday evenings at the classroom of their faculty advisor and Beta Gamma brother, Professor Doug Ashley, on the fourth floor of the College of Charleston's Albert Simons Performing Arts Center. As you know, all KA's are elected by secret ballot."

Knights of the Order

"I remember speaking to the chapter before the ballot would be taken, saying words to this effect: 'Brothers - there comes a time in every man's life - every KA's life - when he is asked to act on the trust he places in another brother. You do not know these five men. But I do. You have to trust your brothers that they are worthy men, deserving of this honor. Just one of you can block their election. The whole Theta Commission project rests in your hands; all of your hands. I can tell you that the whole Order will be waiting to hear what you decide - the Knight Commander, the Councilors, the Executive Director. If you say no, there will be no repercussions. But the project will die. I hope you will put your faith in us and do the right thing."

With that, I left the room and waited in the hall. Five minutes later - five very long minutes, I might add - the door opened and the number IX asked me to come in.

Well, I asked?

"It's done. They're all elected", said the Number I, Charlie Diez with a big grin."

"You done good,boys, I said. And about the part about "no repercussions" - that was all "B.S." You would have had a revote- likely with the Knight Commander sitting on your head. But good for you all. You just made a bunch of new friends."

"The Beta Gamma brothers were all smiles. They knew they had passed a test with flying colors."

Theta Commission was on the way to becoming a reality. The very next day, Brother Diez, the Number I of Beta Gamma, wrote the Executive Director of Kappa Alpha Order that Beta Gamma had approved the initiation of the five men and asking that the Executive Council give its approval. This letter was actually drafted by Brother Varnado, as he wanted it to be delivered quickly to the national office.

In addition to Beta Gamma approval, endorsements were required from the alumnus advisors

The Birth of Theta Commission 2008 - Present

(Brother Rob Varnado and Brother James Elliot), the Province Commander, Brother Randy Smith, and an alumnus at large, (in this case, Brother Brown McLeod). Finally, the Executive Council had to add its approval which it did.

August 1, 2008

Larry Stanton Wiese
Executive Director
Kappa Alpha Order
P.O. Box 1865
115 Liberty Hall Road
Lexington, Virginia 24450

       Re: Petition for Commission Status

Dear Brother Wiese:

       Pursuant to the Constitution and Laws of the Kappa Alpha Order, we respectfully request that the Knight Commander, Executive Council and Advisory Council authorize and grant to us a charter to establish a commission chapter at The Citadel, The Military College of South Carolina, for the purpose of initiating graduates of the Citadel into our Order.

       Of course, if you have any questions, please do not hesitate to contact us. With best fraternal regards, we remain.

                Sincerely,

                Julian V. Brandt III
                Alexander S. Crawford, Jr
                Myron C. Harrington Jr
                James A. W. Rembert
                Hugh B. Tant III

On the evening of April 18, 2008, the Alpha Class of what was to be the Theta Commission was initiated at the Church of the Holy Communion in Charleston, S.C.

By letter dated August 1, 2008, the five new brothers signed a joint letter to Executive Director Wiese asking that they be issued the letter of authorization for a Commission chapter at The Citadel. This request had to be approved by the Advisory and Executive Councils and the Knight Commander.

As noted earlier, after the surrender of the Theta Second charter in 1890, Kappa Alpha Order assigned the name, "Theta" to a new chapter at what would become the University of Kentucky in 1893. It was important that Theta chapter (University of Kentucky) not feel infringed upon by the proposed new Theta Commission (The Citadel).

Accordingly, a meeting was held by the Executive Council and Advisory Council of Kappa Alpha Order on August 8 and 9, 2008, at the Seelbach Hotel, Louisville, KY. to which representatives of Theta chapter at the University of Kentucky were invited. On the first day of the meeting, at the Seelback Hotel, Brother Varnado outlined the process so far. Representatives of Theta chapter at the University of Kentucky were briefed on the proposed Commission. They included Candler Province Commander Taylor, Theta Chapter Alumnus Advisory Committee member Lyn West, and Theta Chapter Number I, Dwight Hammons. The alumni and undergraduate members of Theta Chapter expressed the sentiment that they were honored to be included in the decision and after a recitation of the historical facts, were supportive of the new commission simply being called "Theta Commission".

The following day, after further discussion, Graves Province Commander Randy Smith moved approval by the Advisory Council of the petition to create the Theta Commission at the Citadel. Councilor Russell Brown seconded the motion which passed unanimously.

The next step was to apply to the Knight Commander for a Commission Charter for Theta. That was done and the charter was issued, dated October 3, 2008. In a letter authorizing the issuance of the charter, Knight Commander Duncan made the following finding.

ESTABLISHED 1865

KAPPA ALPHA ORDER

J. Michael Duncan, Knight Commander
5 Rogers Court
Pantego, TX 76013
(214) 886-1865
mikeduncan1865@gmail.com

October 3, 2008

Mr. Larry S. Wiese
Executive Director
Kappa Alpha Order
PO Box 1865
Lexington, VA 24450

Dear Larry,

Thank you for your review of the history of the Theta (Second) Chapter of Kappa Alpha Order that existed at The South Carolina Military Institute (Citadel). I appreciate the thorough research performed by your office into the archives of the Order including the extensive review of the Theta Chapter (Second) records, Convention minutes and relevant issues of the *Kappa Alpha Journal*. Please pass along my thanks to Brent Fellows, Kent McMichael and Councilor Russell Brown for their assistance.

From your review, it appears that Theta (Second) was active as a chapter of the Order beginning in 1883 and was issued a charter by then Knight Commander J.S. Candler. The chapter became inactive in February, 1885, and was revived on February 18, 1887. The charter was never withdrawn by the Order as it likely expected the chapter to resume operations. Theta (Second) was obviously active after 1887, and reported the names of its initiates from 1888-1890, in a November 25, 1890, letter to the Grand Historian of the Order. I also note that the chapter went dormant again in October, 1890, because of general opposition from the Citadel administration to secret societies within the Corps of Cadets.

The 1929 *Directory of Kappa Alpha* details the biographies of approximately 19 Citadel men who were initiated and recorded in the records of the Order as members of Theta (Second) between 1920 and 1921. Some of these men are prominent figures in the history of the Citadel and South Carolina. The records indicate these men were initiated by Beta Gamma chapter at the College of Charleston. I was also interested to learn that the Charleston brothers assisted these Citadel men with the purchase of badges to demonstrate their affiliation with the Order. I believe that this action further indicates a desire on the part of Beta Gamma to assist students at the Citadel in becoming initiated into a dormant KA chapter. I further find that the recent action of Beta Gamma this past Spring, by initiating several Citadel graduates, is yet another instance of Beta Gamma perpetuating the legacy of Theta (Second).

I am convinced by the evidence that I have reviewed that the Order (acting through its General Officers at the time) in approving the initiations of Citadel men through Beta Gamma chapter, was attempting the formation of a Commission much like the Beta Commission at Virginia

Excellence is Our Aim

Military Institute, which was very active during this period. This opinion is further supported by the fact that the charter of Theta (Second) was never officially withdrawn by the General Officers of the Order. To the contrary, they approved the initiations of Citadel men some thirty (30) years after the chapter went dormant for a second time. The point made by both you and Councilor Brown is well taken. Beta Chapter had recently gone through its own issues of opposition by the VMI administration. The VMI brothers, along with the General Officers of the Order, were most creative in their attempts to keep initiating men into Beta despite the restrictions being placed on them by VMI. These Theta (Second) initiations were kept "secret" at the time likely to prevent the effort from being found out by faculty. For whatever reason, the Theta (Second) Commission went dormant after 1921. Executive Vice President Emeritus William E. Forester related to several leaders and members his belief, based on the historical evidence which he knew so well, that a Commission was attempted at Theta (Second) similarly to Beta.

After this review and due consideration, I find that the recent initiation of the five (5) Citadel graduates on April 18, 2008, by Beta Gamma chapter was an act of restoring the Theta (Second) Commission to activity from its period of dormancy since it last acted in 1921. Additionally, it is noteworthy that at its meeting held on August 8, 2008, in Louisville, Kentucky, the Advisory Council passed a unanimous resolution in support of the re-activation of the Theta (Second) Commission.

Accordingly, I declare the Theta (Second) Commission to again be active and that the following five (5) men are appointed as members of that Commission under the authority granted to me by Section 327 of the Constitution of Kappa Alpha Order:

> Mr. Julian V. Brandt, III
> Mr. Alexander S. Crawford, Jr.
> COL Myron C. Harrington, Jr., U.S.M.C. Ret
> COL James A. W. Rembert, U.S.A. Ret
> BG Hugh B. Tant, III, U.S.A. Ret

Further, pursuant to R1-327 (b) & (c), I appoint Brother Rembert as Chairman for the ensuing year. I also appoint Rob Varnado (AA-University of the South '87), A. Donald Evans (ΔT-Francis Marion '76) and the Number I of Beta Gamma chapter as ex-officio members of Theta (Second) Commission to serve in an advisory capacity. Please extend my personal thanks to the brothers of Beta Gamma Chapter for continuing their almost ninety (90) year tradition of assisting the brothers of Theta (Second) Commission.

Fraternally,

J. Michael Duncan
Knight Commander

The official commissioning of Theta and presentation of the charter took place on Friday, March 27, 2009 at 6:00 pm at the Shamrock Room of the Carolina Yacht Club in Charleston, SC. The 38th Knight Commander of Kappa Alpha Order, J. Michael Duncan, presided at the ceremony.

L to R, Baron Fain, Rob Varnado and Don Evans. "The Charleston Three". Photo courtesy of Donald Evans.

The "Charleston Three" celebrated at the Carolina Yacht Club over-looking Charleston Harbor. Guided by Knight Commander Mike Duncan, these three men selected and organized the first group of men comprising the Theta Commission.

Knight Commander J. Michael Duncan(R) presenting the Theta Commission charter to James A. W. Rembert, (center)Chairman on March 27, 2009. Photo courtesy of Donald Evans.

The charter is signed by Knight Commander J. Michael Duncan, the man who set the wheels in motion to establish the Commission in 2007.

The Birth of Theta Commission 2008 - Present

Knight Commander Duncan (front) with Founding Members from L to R, BG Hugh Tant, Vic Brandt, Col. Myron Harrington, Lex Crawford, Col. James Rembert. Photo courtesy of Donald Evans.

The Knight Commander posed with the five original members of Theta Commission after the installation ceremony on March 27, 2009.

Knights of the Order

Beta Class Members, March 27, 2009, L to R, Caldwell Warley, Doug Sass, Ron Plunkett, Selby Richardson, Ted Fetner.(not pictured Luke McBee) Photo courtesy of Donald Evans.

Knight Commander Duncan addressing the group, March 27, 2009. Photo courtesy of Donald Evans.

Knight Commander Duncan presenting the Knight Commander's Accolade to Br. Rob Varnadoe, Photo courtesy of Donald Evans.

The Knight Commander's Accolade, a beautiful medallion of a crimson cross, outlined in gold with a golden knight on horseback centered on it, was established in 1967 to recognize excellence in leadership and service to the Order. It is the highest individual honor an alumnus can receive. It is bestowed in the sole discretion of the Knight Commander and there have been only 178 such awards given in the past 41 years. On Friday, March 27, 2009, in recognition of his leadership in establishing the Theta Commission, Robert B. Varnado was awarded the Knight Commander's Accolade.

Conferral of the
Knight Commander's Accolade
to Robert B. Varnado

The first Knight Commander's Accolades were awarded by then Knight Commander Henry J. Foresman (B-Virginia Military Institute '41) in 1967. He created the award to recognize excellence in leadership and service to the Order and the Executive Council subsequently passed a regulation creating and defining the award as such and stating that the award is given at the sole discretion of the Knight Commander. The Knight Commander's Accolade is the highest individual honor an alumnus can receive. Over the past forty-one years, thirteen Knight Commanders have conferred this high honor on only one-hundred and seventy-eight recipients.

In 1999, Former Knight Commander Idris R. Taylor (ΓX-Texas Tech '70) designed and the Executive Council authorized the creation of a jewel or medallion for this award. The medallion is a crimson cross, outlined in gold, with a golden knight on horseback centered. The jewel hangs from a ribbon collar of crimson and old gold. The jewel/medallion was first presented in 2001.

Tonight, Knight Commander J. Michael Duncan (ΔK-Stephen F. Austin State '69) will add Robert B. Varnado to this roll of honor by conferring on him the Knight Commander's Accolade.

Robert B. Varnado

Rob attended the University of the South and was initiated into Alpha Alpha chapter in 1987 where he served as Rush Chairman, III and IX. Upon graduation from the University of the South, Rob attended the University of South Carolina School of Law. Rob is currently the senior partner and managing member of the Varnado Law Firm in Mount Pleasant, South Carolina. He has served as an officer in the Charleston Alumni Chapter and was appointed as Graves Deputy Province Commander for Academic Affairs in 2008.

For his exceptional work in establishing the Theta Commission, Knight Commander J. Michael Duncan appointed him as an ex-officio member of the Commission.

The Birth of Theta Commission 2008 - Present

Asked why they accepted the invitation to join Kappa Alpha Order, the Founding Members had this to say,

Colonel James A.W. Rembert:

"When I was a junior in high school, my brother was entering the University of South Carolina. I got an earful about which was the best fraternity at USC at the time, KA or SAE. Some of his friends joined SAE, but I liked the ones who with my brother joined KA. I liked the Southern Gentleman part of it, the flag and the ball. I wanted to go to the University of the South at Sewanee as an Episcopal KA Gentleman. My father, for cause, sent me to The Citadel where I became for a while one of Orwell's rough men standing ready to do violence on behalf of those who would do us harm. When the call came asking if I would like to be in the Theta Commission of KAO, the dream after fifty years came true."

Colonel Myron Harrington:

"My first thoughts when I was approached to be an original/charter member to resurrect the Kappa Alpha Order/Theta Commission at The Citadel were of bewilderment and wonderment. My Bewilderment was to why I was identified and wonderment in the special effort being made by the Order to restore The Citadel to the rolls. As I learned more about the history of the Order at the college and its overall history the more intrigued and interested I became because I saw the many parallels it had with the principles and values of The Citadel. Within a short period of time I became convinced that re-establishing the Commission would be a good thing and I agreed to commit to membership. Also, the fact that I had a great grandfather who fought for the Confederate cause along with our spiritual founder, Robert E. Lee, further solidified my desire to have this connection with the past.

My bewilderment and wonderment turned to pride, humbleness and honor as I was initiated as a KA. I then discovered to my delight that I had several family members that were KAs.

In essence, I believe that most Citadel men especially those of southern upbringing will find that membership in KA will be a reminder to remember the words of General Lee that we saw everyday while a cadet. "Duty then is the sublimest word in our language. Do your duty in all things. You cannot do more; you should never wish to do less."

That is what I try to do every day, sometime I succeed and sometime I fail."

Brigadier General Hugh Tant:

"Having long been inspired by the life of General Robert E. Lee and his timeless words, "Duty is the sublimest word in the English language," I knew that Kappa Alpha Order was in my heart. Furthermore, I was deeply impressed by two very good friends who were members of the Order, Doug Bostick and Henry Siegling, whose boundless love of KA was so genuine, that I knew Kappa Alpha Order was for me. The opportunity to be a part of this Order and to bring fellow worthy Citadel alumni into membership was unquestionably the right thing to do."

Lex Crawford:

"When you study and read about the Kappa Alpha Order, and start to understand it; on initiation it becomes one of the driving forces of your life, just as your religion or family. It is also a natural extension of The Citadel experience."

Vic Brandt:

"As a Cadet, I knew about the Kappa Alpha Order and their legendary history with General Lee at Washington and Lee and later VMI. I was also keenly aware of the "no fraternity" rule at the Citadel. The closest thing resembling a fraternity I belonged to as a Cadet was the Calliopean Literary Society founded in 1845. The role models for the Calliopean were Washington and Calhoun.

The Birth of Theta Commission 2008 - Present

I had high school classmates who were KA's and knew we cadets were missing an opportunity. I regularly had lunch with Don Evans, Baron Fain, Richard Hyman and Rob Varnado, all members of the Kappa Alpha Order. I knew from their reports that the KA tradition was alive and well in Charleston.

I knew something was up when Don Evans and Rob Varnado wanted to have a private conversation with me. I was shocked and honored to learn that they had been working with the national leadership of KA to re-institute a relationship with the Kappa Alpha Order through creation of the Theta Commission. I was asked to be one of the five founding members of the Commission. At once, I began to research The Kappa Alpha Order and studied the Varlet. I was totally unaware of the rich history KA had at The Citadel. There were many things that impressed me about KA and the effect it can have on forming a young man's character by emphasizing the code of Chivalry. The personal qualities and codes of conduct that KA holds as standards are so missing in today's society. It is my hope that by continuing the KA legacy at the Citadel, quality and gentlemanly conduct and that sense of "Noblesse Oblige" will continue for generations to come.

Membership in the Order is both an honor and obligation. The honor is evident to be included in such an accomplished and noteworthy fraternity of men. The obligation, is to practice the code of conduct and be a role model for those who follow in the «long gray line»."

Of their critical role in selecting the founding members and helping launch Theta Commission, the "Charleston Three" had this to say,

Robert Varnado:

"Were two institutions ever made for each other more than The Citadel and the Kappa Alpha Order? Do two mottoes sum up all the manly virtues of chivalry than "Duty, Honor, Country" and "Dieu et les Dames?" To have played a very small role in reuniting these two venerable organizations is my proudest moment as a KA."

Knights of the Order

Baron Fain :

"Kappa Alpha Order's founding generation wanted our fraternity at The Citadel. It was no less natural a choice than Beta at VMI. The Citadel's martial values of duty, honor and patriotism combined with its enduring Southern culture of reverence and gentility was and remains an ideal community in which Kappa Alpha could thrive. The challenge would always be the necessary restrictions of cohesive discipline in the Corps of Cadets. However the surrounding faculty/ graduate, Charleston and South Carolina communities offered ample populations to nurture an active commission. As the opportunity to institute a Commission there was considered, we soon recognized we had the fraternal experience and social networks necessary to build an authentic cadre devoted to each comple- mentary tradition in Kappa Alpha and The Citadel. We shared with our first class of candidates proven devotion in church, country, heritage and gentility. The combined experience, stature and character of the men we pledged to our cause entirely captured the chivalry we knew Kappa Alpha champions. If our Order holds that we do not make KAs but rather discover them, the question remained whether we could offer something to mature alumni or graduating cadets that they did not already possess. The answer lay in the beautiful legacy of our customs, as they have continued to inspire and sustain generations of our brethren through- out the Order. The Citadel KAs desired no less than what we still share - an authentic and enduring fellowship founded by the example of Robert E. Lee, our spiritual founder.

Don and Rob were and remain among my closest friends and brothers in Christ. To share our cherished Order with Citadel men whom I count no less esteemed or beloved has been a most profound honor. It is pleasure and a privilege to be in their company and Kappa Alpha has been blessed for it."

Donald Evans:

"Being part of the re-chartering and success of the Kappa Alpha Order's Theta commission is one of my proudest achievements. My reconnection with the Corps

The Birth of Theta Commission 2008 - Present

through the introduction of the Order has been most gratifying. Our founders would be as pleased as I am with the caliber of Theta Commission's brothers."

Since the initiation of the Alpha Class of Theta Commission on April 18, 2008, the organization has grown dramatically. The classes, date initiated and their size are as follows:

Alpha Class, April 18, 2008, five members
Beta Class, March 19, 2009, seven members
Gamma Class, November 10, 2009, eleven members
Delta Class, May 8, 2010, 34 members
Epsilon Class, May 8, 2010, 27 members
Zeta Class, May 7, 2011, 24 members
Eta Class, May 7, 2011, 32 members
Theta Class, May 5, 2012, 31 members
Iota Class, May 5, 2012, 42 members
Kappa Class, May 4, 2013, 31 members
Lambda Class, May 4, 2013, 42 members
Mu Class, May 10, 2014, 46 members
Nu Class, May 10, 2014, 66 members
Xi Class, May 9, 2015, 34 members
Omicron Class, May 9, 2015, 59 members
Pi Class, May 7, 2016, 33 members
Rho Class, May 7, 2016, 31 members

Theta Commission membership meetings are held four times a year with a fifth formal event known as a Convivium, including our Kappa Alpha Roses, on Robert E. Lee's birthday in January. Each meeting includes a social hour followed by an evening dinner. The business meetings are semi-formal affairs at which strict Kappa Alpha meeting protocol is followed. The President, or Number I, chairs the meeting, during which reports are received from each of the various officers

of the Commission.

Theta Commission decided early on that part of its mission was to support The Citadel in general and its graduates in particular. Accordingly, a Service Committee was established under the leadership of Brigadier General Hugh B. Tant, III. General Tant's committee embarked on two projects.

Realizing that our country had many Citadel graduates deployed to Iraq and Afghanistan as well as other places around the globe, General Tant and his committee organized the sending of quarterly "care" packages to those deployed as well as men under their command. Thus far, four deployed brothers have received quarterly care packages for themselves and men and women under their command.

The Service Committee also established a mentoring program. The goal of this program is to link young graduates with older Kappa Alpha Brothers in their chosen profession. The older brothers act as mentors, providing advice, connections, contacts and guidance to these recent graduates just starting out in the business world. So far, six brothers have been mentored in this program.

Graduation Day at The Citadel is a day of joy and happiness for both graduating cadets and their families. Members of the graduating class selected for membership in Kappa Alpha Order leave The Citadel after receiving their diplomas and arrive at St. Philip's Church with their family members. There they are provided a lunch in the Church Parish House. After lunch, they form up for what will be their last march in their cadet uniforms into the church for the initiation ceremony. They are led into the church by a Citadel bagpiper for the solemn, private ceremony.

The families are present during the induction portion of the initiation

ceremony. After a brief intermission, the initiation ceremony takes place. Theta Commission has been fortunate to have Kappa Alpha brothers from the National Administrative Office conduct each initiation since 2010.

Theta Commission now numbers over 500 members with approximately 75 alumni and day- of graduates being initiated each year. But numbers do not tell the whole story. Quality is more important. Like their predecessors of the previous two centuries, the men of Theta Commission are men of substance and accomplishment. Those traits are underpinned by deep religious faith and a commitment of service to their fellow man. Each man endeavors to live the highest tradition of "Excelsior".

These men range from young men in the dawn of their lives to older men in the twilight of their years, from a retired Bishop to a parish Priest, from recently commissioned Second Lieutenants to retired three star Generals, from everyday businessmen to Chief Executive Officers, from Lawyers to Judges.

The Citadel itself is represented by two former Presidents, over half dozen present or former members of the Board of Visitors, several present or former tactical officers, a half dozen present or former faculty members and numerous administrators.

Given this success, Theta Commission might well be called a "Banner" chapter as William Edward Dick, a founding member, described Theta Chapter in the 1880's. How the Commission will evolve in the years to come is up to future generations. Suffice it to say, its foundation is strong, its mission is clear, its goal is worthy and its history is now recorded.

Knights of the Order

Conferral of the Knight Commander's Accolade

The Knight Commander's Accolade is the highest individual honor an alumnus can receive. It is awarded at the exclusive discretion of the Knight Commander. Over the Order's 150 year history just 217 recipients have been so honored.

In a surprise visit to Charleston on Saturday, May 9, 2015, Knight Commander William B. Dreyer awarded the Knight Commander's Accolade to Colonel James A. W. Rembert. Colonel Rembert was the original Chairman of Theta Commission and served for seven years in that capacity as well as President of the organization. It was largely due to his inspiring and unfailing leadership that Theta Commission has been so successful.

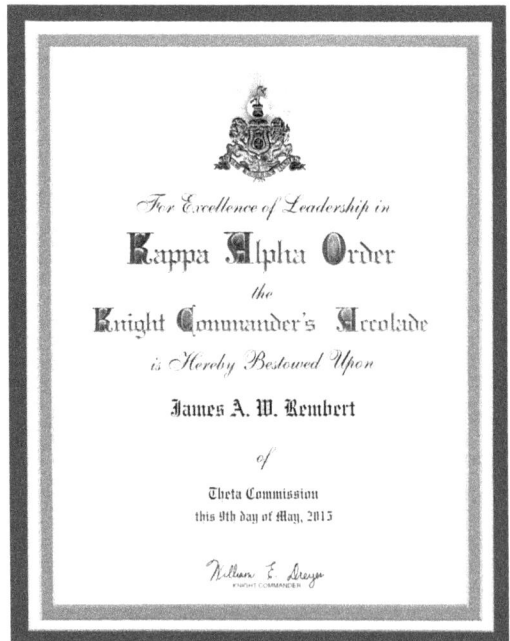

For Excellence of Leadership in

Kappa Alpha Order

the

Knight Commander's Accolade

is Hereby Bestowed Upon

James A. W. Rembert

of

Theta Commission
this 9th day of May, 2015

William E. Dreyer
KNIGHT COMMANDER

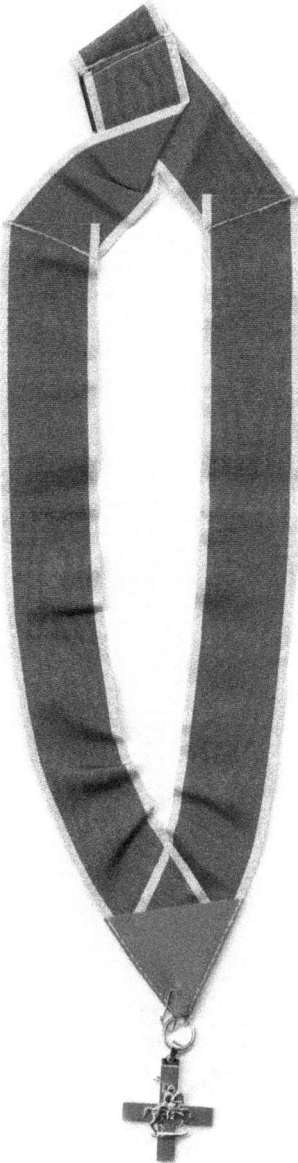

The first Knight Commander's Accolades were awarded by then Knight Commander Henry J. Foresman (Beta Commission – VMI '41) in 1967. He created the award to recognize excellence in leadership and service to the Order. The Executive Council subsequently passed a regulation creating and defining the award as such and stating that the award is given at the sole discretion of the Knight Commander.

Knights of the Order

Book Presentation to The Citadel President

Author, Thomas Dewey Wise presenting his book "Knights of the Order" to General John Rosa.

On August 28, 2014, a ceremony was held in the office of the President of The Citadel. The President was presented with a copy of Knights of the Order, a History of Kappa Alpha Order at The Citadel 1883-2013.

From l. to r., General John Rosa, General Clifton Poole, Thomas Dewey Wise, Colonel James Rembert, and Ron Plunkett.

THETA COMMISSION BROTHERS WHO HAVE
SERVED ON THE CITADEL BOARD OF VISITORS

Col. Myron Charles Harrington, Jr., '60

Col. Francis Palmer Mood, '60 (former Chairman)

Col. Robert Hucks Nuttall, '62

Col. Lewis Eugene Pinson, '72

Col. Fred Lewis Price, Jr., '75 (Vice Chairman)

Col. Glenn D. Addison, '79 (former Vice Chairman)

Col. John Andrew McAllister, Jr., '80

Col. Dylan Ward Goff, '02

Sen. Thomas Dewey Wise, x'61

Knights of the Order

THETA COMMISSION FLAG OFFICERS

Theta Commission is proud to count among its members, 11 men who achieved Flag Officer rank in the military service

Gen. William Oscar Brice, Jr., '21, Marines

Lt. Gen. Ellie Givans Shuler, Jr., '51, Air Force

Lt. Gen. Colby Marshall Broadwater, '72, Army

Maj. Gen. Orlando Clarendon Mood, '21, Army

Maj. Gen. Roger Clifton Poole, '59, Army

Maj. Gen. Francis Eli Wishart, Jr., '63, SC State Guard

Maj. Gen. Nathaniel Heyward Robb, Jr., '64, NC National Guard

Maj. Gen. James Edward Lockemy, '71, SC Military Department, JSD

Brig. Gen. James Emory Mace, '63, Army

Brig. Gen. Hugh Banks Tant, Jr., '71, Army

Brig. Gen. Gregory Neil Walters, '87, SC Air National Guard

DISTINGUISHED THETA COMMISSION BROTHERS WHO HAVE BEEN RECOGNIZED FOR COMBAT VALOR AND WHO ARE THE CITADEL'S MOST HIGHLY DECORATED LIVING GRADUATES.

Brigadier General Emory Mace, '63, USA, received the Army's second highest award for valor, the Distinguished Service Cross, and the third highest award for valor, the Silver Star, in Vietnam.

Colonel Myron Harrington, '60, USMC, received the Navy's second highest award for valor, the Navy Cross, and the third highest award for valor, the Silver Star, in Vietnam.

9th Knight Commander
John Temple Graves (1856-1925)

John Temple Graves wrote and presented the immortal toast (now given each year at Convivium) that named Robert E. Lee Kappa Alpha's Spiritual Founder and S. Z. Ammen its Practical Founder. He was born in Abbeville County, South Carolina, in 1856 and initiated by Gamma Chapter in 1871. He served as Grand Historian during his predecessor's two terms. Elected as Knight Commander on July 27, 1881, he served through October of that year when he resigned. Graves also was president of the 1877 and 1881 conventions and orator of the Sixteenth Convention in 1891. An editor or editorial director of nineteen papers, Graves was best known as a lecturer and speaker. President Grover Cleveland once proclaimed, "Graves is the most brilliant and statesmen-like orator heard in New York in years." Graves died in Washington, D.C., on August 8, 1925, and was buried in Atlanta.

Prior Knight Commander *Daniel Rowell Neal, Jr.*

Next Knight Commander *John Slaughter Candler*

Copyright © 2014 Kappa Alpha Order

The Birth of Theta Commission 2008 - Present

Theta Commission is a member of Graves Province of Kappa Alpha Order which includes the entire State of South Carolina. Each year, Graves Province inducts one member from each chapter into its Court of Honor.

The criteria for being inducted into the Court of Honor are as follows:

Members of the Court shall be loyal, interested alumni of the Order who have been out out of undergraduate school and not affliated with an Active Chapter (as an active member) for at least three years, who have distinguished themselves by continuing service to and interest in the Order, its Active Chapters, Commissions or Alumni Chapters, or who have brought credit to themselves and to the Order in their public or private lives. Members need not be residents of Graves Province or an Alumnus of a Graves Province Chapter or Commission.

This accolade is in recognition of the member's meritorious service to the Order. Past honorees of this award are:

Colonel James A.W. Rembert - 2010

Ronald C. Plunkett - 2011

Edward H. Fetner, III - 2012

Thomas Dewey Wise - 2013

Brigadier General Hugh B.Tant, III - 2014

Major General R. Clifton Poole - 2015

Colonel John G. Lackey-2016

Knights of the Order

APPENDIX

Knights of the Order

THETA SECOND INITIATES 1883-1890

There were 43 men initiated during the 1883-1890 time period. The years and the number of men initiated are as follows:

1883-5

1884-7

1885-0

1886-0

1887-15

1888-8

1889-6

1890-2

Total 43

THETA SECOND 1883 INITIATES

WILLIAM EDWARD DICK

Born, Sumter, S.C., December 19, 1864, entered The Citadel, October, 1882, Pay Cadet, initiated into Kappa Alpha, 1883. Charter member of Theta Second, first member initiated into Theta Second. Graduated from the Citadel, 1886. He married Anna Francis Blanding, November 12, 1890. He was engaged in farming all his life. He died on September 13, 1916 and is buried at St. Philips Episcopal Church, Bradford Springs, Lee County, S.C.

FRANCIS OVID SPAIN

Born, Darlington, S.C., July 29, 1866, entered The Citadel, 1882, Beneficiary Cadet, initiated into Kappa Alpha, 1883, Charter Member of Theta Second, graduated from The Citadel, 1886 with a Bachelor of Science degree. Episcopalian. He married Jean Grant Spain. Assistant Professor of Mathematics, Georgia School of Technology, Later, he was President of Bankers Financing Co. and Bankers Trading Co. in Jacksonville, FL. He also was Manager of the City Electric & Water Department for the City of Jacksonville. He died on June 17, 1941 and is buried at Grove Hill Cemetery, Darlington, S.C.

PAUL HOUT TAMPLET

Born, Georgetown, S.C., 1863, entered The Citadel, 1882, Beneficiary Cadet, initiated into Kappa Alpha, 1883, Charter Member of Theta Second, Held the position of President (I) in the chapter. Mason. He married Gertrude N. Tamplet in 1899. In 1920, he was living in Washington, D.C. and employed as a General Agent for Mutual Benefit Life Insurance Co. He died on October 13, 1924 and is buried in Washington, D.C.

ARMSTRONG JOLLY HOWARD

Born, Darlington, S.C., May 6, 1866, entered The Citadel, 1882, Beneficiary Cadet, initiated into Kappa Alpha, 1883. He married May E. Howard in 1896. He was a farmer in Darlington County. He died at age 59 on July 19, 1925. He is buried at Grove Hill Cemetery, Darlington, S.C. His son, Armstrong Jolly Howard, Jr. graduated from The Citadel, Class of 1923. Howard, Jr. did not follow his father and join Kappa Alpha Order. Perhaps its existence was unknown to him in the 1920's.

WILLIAM JENNINGS

Born, Pendleton, S.C., 1863, entered The Citadel, 1882, Beneficiary Cadet, initiated into Kappa Alpha, 1883, Adjunct Professor of Mathematics at Georgia School of Technology. He died in Atlanta, GA, on March 10, 1908. He was survived by a wife and 7 year old daughter. He is buried in Magnolia Cemetery, Charleston, S.C.

KENNETH GORDON MATHESON

Born, Cheraw, S.C., July 28, 1864, entered The Citadel, 1882, Beneficiary Cadet, initiated into Kappa Alpha, 1883, A.M., LL.D., Sc.D, Mason. He married Belle Seddon Fleet. After graduating from The Citadel in 1885, he became Commandant of Cadets at Georgia Military College until 1888. Later, he taught at the University of Tennessee and Missouri Military Academy. In 1896, he entered Stanford University and earned his Mas-

Kenneth Gordon Matheson

175

ter's degree in English. He continued his teaching career at Georgia School of Technology (now known as Georgia Tech) in 1897. Matheson was elected President of the school in 1906 and served until 1922. In 1922, he was elected president of Drexel Institute of Art, Science and Industry, now known as Drexel University. He formally retired in 1931, but continued teaching until his death on November 29, 1931. He is buried at Old Saint David's Episcopal Church Cemetery in Cheraw, S.C.

THETA SECOND 1884 INITIATES

COUNCIL BLACK ASHLEY

Born, Barnwell County, S.C., November 1, 1864, entered The Citadel, 1883, Pay Cadet, initiated 1884, A.B. degree with Honors in 1887. He was President of the chapter (I). He married Cora Parramore and was a prominent attorney in Madison, FL having been admitted to the Bar on October 9, 1888. He was shot and killed in front of his law office on November 18, 1909. He is buried in Oak Ridge Cemetery, Madison, Fla.

GEORGE MORRALL GADSDEN

Born, Charleston, S.C., October 19, 1865, entered The Citadel, 1882, Pay Cadet, initiated, 1884, Married, Leona Guerard Gadsden. He was Director of Public Works, Savannah, Georgia. He died on April 14, 1925 and is buried at Bonaventure Cemetery, Savannah, Ga.

THOMAS PERRIN HARRISON

Born, Abbeville, S.C., October 11, 1864, entered The Citadel, 1882, Beneficiary Cadet, initiated, 1884, Presbyterian, B.S. degree. Second Honor Graduate, 1886. Taught English at The Citadel 1886-1888. He married Adelia Leftwich Harrison in 1894. Dean, N.C. College of Agriculture and Engineering (now N.C. State).Ph. D. in English, Johns Hopkins University, 1891. Oldest living graduate of the Citadel, 1930, Mason, Professor. Wrote articles on many literary topics. He died on November 1, 1949 and is buried in Roberts Presbyterian Church Cemetery, Anderson, S.C. Thomas Perrin Harrison received an Honorary Doctor of Laws degree from The Citadel in 1930.

Thomas Perrin Harrison,

Courtesy: The Citadel Archives & Museum, Charleston, SC.

FRANCIS PARKER HUGER

Born, Charleston, SC, August 1, 1867, entered The Citadel, 1882, Pay Cadet, initiated, 1884. Real Estate business. Resided in New York, New York.

EVANDER McIVAR LAW, JR.

Born, Columbia, S.C. 1866, entered The Citadel, 1882, Beneficiary Cadet, initiated into Kappa Alpha, 1884, Graduated, July 28, 1886. C.E.E.E., Civil Engineer, Professor, Chemistry and Physics, South Florida Military Academy. He later attended and graduated from both dental and medical school. He received his medical degree from the Maryland Medical College in Baltimore, MD in 1903. He died on

March 9, 1922. At the time of his death, he was a practicing medical doctor in Miami, Fl. He was accidentally killed after coming in contact with a high voltage wire. He was 56 years old at the time of his death. He is buried in Oak Hill Cemetery, Bartow, FL. He was the son of Major General Evander Law, CSA, Class of 1856.

BENJAMIN A. MUNNERLYN, Jr.

Born, Georgetown, S.C., December 19, 1867, entered The Citadel, 1882, Pay Cadet, initiated into Kappa Alpha, 1884, First Honor Graduate, 1886. He died at age 26 in an accident in Savannah, GA on March 17, 1893. He was superintending some work when he was struck in the head by a pile-driver. He is buried at Prince George Winyah Cemetery, Georgetown, S.C.

Benjamin A. Munnerlyn, Jr.,
Courtesy: The Citadel Archives & Museum, Charleston, SC.

EDWARD FROST PARKER

Born, Charleston, S.C., December 16,1867, entered The Citadel, 1883, Pay Cadet, initiated, 1884, Transferred to Lambda, (University of Virginia), M.D. First Honor Graduate from medical school.

Professor of Medicine, S.C. Medical College, Physician, specializing in Eye, Ear, Nose and Throat. Married Harriett Horry Frost. Died, March 28, 1938. He is buried in Magnolia Cemetery, Charleston, S.C.

Edward Frost Parker,
Courtesy: The Citadel Archives & Museum, Charleston, SC

THETA SECOND 1887 INITIATES

GEORGE WILLIAMS ALLISON

George W. Allison,
Courtesy: The Citadel Archives & Museum
(Note KA pin on Cadet blouse)

Born November 5, 1870, Lancaster S.C. entered The Citadel in 1886, Beneficiary Cadet, initiated into Kappa Alpha Order, 1887. B.S. degree. He taught school in South Carolina for 3 years after graduation in 1890. He then went to Washington, DC where he was a private secretary to a Member of Congress and later a U.S. Senator. While in Washington, he attended Georgetown University earning both LL.B and LL.M. degrees. After leaving Washington, he went to California where he was Chief Clerk and the Purchasing Agent for the Northwestern Railroad. He died on November 15, 1928 at age 57 and is buried in West Side Cemetery, Lancaster, S.C.

WILLIAM BENJAMIN DAVIS

Born, Jacksonville, Fla. September 4, 1869, entered The Citadel, 1886, Pay Cadet, initiated 1887, Baptist, Grand Chancellor, K.P. 28, Married, Julia Mosely Davis. He was employed as a druggist in Madison, Fla. He died on October 15, 1941 and is buried in Madison, Fla.

WILLIAM WOODWARD DIXON

Born Woodward, S.C., 1868, entered The Citadel, 1886, Beneficiary

Cadet, initiated 1887. He was President of the chapter (I) in 1888, Delegate, 14th Kappa Alpha Convention 1887. Lawyer and U.S. Commissioner. He was Commandant of Virginia Military Prep School for a time. He practiced law in Winnsboro, S.C. He served one term (1915-1916) in the South Carolina House of Representatives. He died on October 1, 1944 and is buried in Ridgeway Cemetery in Fairfield County, S.C.

RANDOLPH BRADFORD DUNBAR

Born, Beech Island, S.C., February 27, 1869, entered The Citadel, 1886, Pay Cadet, initiated 1887. Married, Ruth Alma Simkins on January 20, 1892. He inherited Rose Hill Plantation and was a farmer. He died on August 11, 1957 and is buried at Hammond Cemetery, Beech Island, S.C.

JAMES LENNERTON FERGUSON

Born, Charleston, S.C., April 15, 1868, entered The Citadel, 1886, Pay Cadet, initiated 1887, Presbyterian, Shriner. Married, Effie Sheron Ferguson. He was employed as a Cotton broker/ bookkeeper. He died on January 12, 1934 and is buried in Magnolia Cemetery, Charleston, S.C.

RICHARD WOODWARD HUTSON

Born, Yemassee, S.C., August, 14, 1869, entered The Citadel, 1886, Pay Cadet, initiated into Kappa Alpha, 1887, Presbyterian. He married Myra Jenkins Hutson. Clerk, U.S. District Court, Eastern District of S.C. (1902-1939). Succeeded his father, Charles J.C. Hudson who had been Clerk before him. Descendant of Charleston's first mayor, Richard Hutson. He died in Charleston on January 29, 1939 and is buried at Stoney Creek Cemetery, Beaufort, S.C.

Knights of the Order

BEATIE ANDREW INGLIS

Born, Madison, Fla., April 20,1871, entered The Citadel, 1886, Pay Cadet, initiated 1887, Masters in Engineering from Stevens Institute. He married, Catherine L. Inglis in 1899. Superintendent, Florida Manufacturing Co. He died on May 20, 1933 and is buried in Oak Ridge Cemetery, Madison, Fla.

GEORGE YUILLE MacMURPHY

Born, Augusta, Ga., March 10, 1869, entered The Citadel, 1886, Pay Cadet, initiated into Kappa Alpha, 1887, Transferred to Chi,(Vanderbilt University) M.D. Physician, practicing in Charleston, S.C. He died on February 13, 1951 and is buried in Magnolia Cemetery, Augusta, Ga.

WILLIAM EPHRIAM MIKELL

Born, Sumter, S.C., January 28, 1868, entered The Citadel, 1886, Beneficiary Cadet, initiated 1887, Episcopal, B.S. , LL.M.,LL.D, D.C.L., Delegate, 14th Convention in 1889, Dean, University of Pennsylvania Law School, Professor. He taught at the University of Pennsylvania School of Law for 46 years. He wrote a book in 1908 entitled "Cases in Criminal Law" and dedicated it "To my classmates, Archibald Gilchrist Singletary and Frank Barron Grier, The one learned in the Civil and the other in the Common Law". "In appreciation for their long and valued friendship." He married Martha Turner McBee. He died on January 20, 1944 and is buried on Edisto Island, S.C.

HUTSON COLCOCK MOORE

Born, York, S.C., 1868, entered The Citadel, 1886, Beneficiary Cadet, initiated, 1887, Cotton Broker. He died in 1927 and is buried at Clarksville Cemetery, Clarksville, Tx.

RICHARD WILSON RILEY

Born, Hayes Crossroads near Barnwell, S.C., October 26, 1867, entered The Citadel, 1886, Pay Cadet, initiated, 1887, Baptist, He had attended the Old Yorkville Academy and after two years at The Citadel, he left to obtain his DMD degree from the University of Maryland. Dentist, Married, Anneta Dowling Simms (first marriage), Lula Mae Roberts (second marriage) in 1912. He died on September 30, 1922 and is buried at Cave Methodist Church Cemetery, Allendale, S.C.

JENKINS MIKELL ROBERTSON

Born, Charleston, S.C., December 26, 1872, entered The Citadel, 1887, Pay Cadet, initiated, 1887, Episcopal, Fertilizer Merchant. Married, Virginia Brawley Robertson. He lived at 166 Broad St. in Charleston. He died on April 14, 1952 and is buried at Magnolia Cemetery, Charleston, S.C.

WILLIAM HOWE SIMONS

Born, Charleston, S.C., July 31,1869, entered The Citadel, 1886, Beneficiary Cadet, initiated, 1887, First Honor Graduate, 1890,wounded in the Spanish-American War, 1904-1908, Commandant of Cadets, Professor of Military Science and Tactics at the Citadel, Promoted to Major, June, 1917, Lt. Col. in July, 1917, and Colonel on August 16, 1917. Commanded 327th Infantry Regiment, died April, 12, 1918, at Camp Gordon, Ga. Buried at St. Paul's Episcopal Church Cemetery, Summerville, S.C. A window in the Summerall Chapel is named in his honor.

ARCHIBALD GILCHRIST SINGLETARY

Born, Marion, S.C., November 15, 1867, entered The Citadel, 1886,

Beneficiary Cadet, initiated into Kappa Alpha Order, 1887, served as President (I), Episcopal, B.S. degree, Mason, Married Evalon Bryan Singletary. Insurance agent in Louisiana. Died, November 27, 1936 in Point Coulee, La.

ERNEST RUSSELL ZEMP

Born, Camden, S.C., May 25,1871, entered The Citadel, 1886, Pay Cadet, initiated into Kappa Alpha Order, 1887, B.S. degree, Methodist,. Married, Kathleen H. Zemp in 1899. Medical Doctor (Obstetrican), Elk, President, Tennessee Medical Association. He died in Knoxville, Tenn. on February 7, 1954, at age 83, of a heart attack.

A.G. Singletary,
Courtesy: The Citadel Archives & Museum, Charleston, SC

THETA SECOND 1888 INITIATES

ROBERT BRODIE JONES

Born, Mobile, AL., 1870, entered The Citadel, 1886, Pay Cadet, initiated into Kappa Alpha, 1888, died, 1897

JOHN LAKE

Born, Edgefield, S.C., June 11,1870, entered The Citadel, 1887, Beneficiary Cadet, initiated into Kappa Alpha, 1888, Honorably discharged from The Citadel in 1890, one year prior to graduating because of bad eyesight. He attended the Columbia Theological Seminary and the Southern Baptist Theological Seminary. He became a Missionary to China, where he founded the Tai-Kam Leper Hospital. He married Pearl Hall Williams in 1907, Elford Bostick in 1909 and Virginia Barclay in 1933. On June 2, 1930, he received Honorary Doctor of Law degree from The Citadel. He died on August 29, 1949 and is buried in Edgefield,

John Lake,
Courtesy: The Citadel Archives & Museum, Charleston, SC.

S.C. There is a bronze historical marker located near Edgefield in his honor.

JAMES FRANCIS McELWEE

Born, October 29, 1869 at York, S.C., entered The Citadel, 1888, Beneficiary Cadet, initiated 1888, Traveling Salesman. Married Florence Moore Allison on June 15, 1898. He died on February 18, 1958 and is buried in Rose Hill Cemetery, York, S.C.

James Francis McElwee,
Courtesy: The Citadel Archives & Museum, Charleston, SC

Joseph W. Magrath,
Courtesy: The Citadel Archives and Museum, Charleston, SC
(Note KA pin on Cadet blouse)

JOSEPH WALKER MAGRATH

Born, Charleston, S.C. February 5, 1872, entered The Citadel, 1887, Pay Cadet, initiated into Kappa Alpha, 1888, B.S. degree, Episcopal, Lawyer. He married Rachel Ann Rapalie Magrath. He lived in New York City for most of his life. He died in 1949 and is buried in Magnolia Cemetery, Charleston, S.C.

THOMAS JOAB MAULDIN

Born, Pickens, S.C., July 21, 1870, entered The Citadel, 1887, Beneficiary Cadet, initiated into Kappa Alpha, 1888, Graduated from The Citadel in 1891 as 2nd Honor Graduate and was admitted to the S.C. bar in 1892. He taught school for a number of years and was Principal of the Laurens Male Academy. He married Francis Miles Hagood in September, 1904. He served in the S.C. House of Representatives during 1905-1906 term. He served in the South Carolina Senate from 1908 to 1912. For a brief period, he was editor of the Pickens Journal. He was elected a Circuit Court Judge in 1912 and served until his death on October 22, 1931. A window in Summerall Chapel is named in his honor. (See his home in Memoralibia),

JOHN FINLAYSON MAYS

Born, Jefferson County, Fla., February 14, 1869, entered The Citadel, 1886, Pay Cadet, initiated 1888. Farmer. He married Elizabeth Brooks Turnbull. He died on May 22, 1927 and is buried in Roseland Cemetery, Monticello, Fla.

NEWTON PINCKNEY WALKER

Born, Cedar Springs, S.C., 1872, entered The Citadel, 1888, Pay Cadet, initiated, 1888, Transferred to Lambda Chapter, (University of Virginia). He was only 23 years old when he died in 1895. Newton Pinckney Walker is buried at Oakwood Cemetery in Spartanburg, S.C.

EPHRIAM MIKELL WHALEY

Born, Edisto Island, S.C., February 27,1871, entered The Citadel, 1888, Pay Cadet, initiated into Kappa Alpha Order, 1888, Graduated from the Medical College of South Carolina in 1896. Medical Doctor. Mason. Episcopalian. He married Cecile S. Inglesby Whaley in 1897.

He practiced eye, ear, nose and throat medicine in Columbia, S.C. for many years. Dr. Whaley owned one of the first automobiles in the City of Columbia. He was a prominent citizen of Columbia, his obituary meriting front page coverage in *The State* newspaper. He died on December 27, 1926 at age 86. His funeral services were conducted by Rev. Kirkman George Finlay, the Bishop of the Episcopal Diocese of Upper South Carolina and he is buried in Elmwood Cemetery, Columbia, S.C.

THETA SECOND 1889 INITIATES

WILLIAM BICELL DANIELS

Born, Burke County, GA. February 19, 1872, entered The Citadel, 1889, Pay Cadet, initiated, 1889, Knights of Pythis. Wholesale Grocery Broker. He married, Mary Martha Daniels in 1893. He died on February 26, 1942 and is buried at Magnolia Cemetery, Augusta, Ga.

FRANK BARRON GRIER

Born, York, S.C., December 10, 1869, entered The Citadel, (xx), Beneficiary Cadet, initiated 1889, A.B. degree. He later received an Honorary LL.D degree from The Citadel. Shriner, Lawyer. He married Retta McWillie Withers. He practiced law in Greenwood for most of his career. A window in the Summerall Chapel is dedicated in his honor. He died on December 2, 1933 and is buried in Elmwood Cemetery, Columbia, S.C. Frank Barron Grier received an Honorary Doctor of Law degree from the Citadel in 1933.

JOHN RATCHFORD HART

Born, York, S.C., April 20, 1873, entered The Citadel, 1889, Pay Cadet, initiated, 1889, Shriner, Lawyer. He married Mary Jackson Hunter Hart, June 6, 1906. He died June 22, 1939 and is buried at Rose Hill Cemetery, York, S.C.

PETER KEYS McCULLY

Born, Anderson, S.C., January 18, 1873, entered The Citadel, 1887, Pay Cadet, initiated into Kappa Alpha, 1889, Best Drilled Cadet, 1889(Star of the West Medal not begun until 1893), Presbyterian, Cotton Broker, Married, Margaret Fretwell McCully. Colonel, Commander of the 118th Infantry Regiment, National Guard, World

War I. Father was a cadet at the Citadel at outbreak of Civil War and fought in the Battalion of Cadets. His son, Robert H. Mc-Cully, was also a Citadel graduate. Died, June 8, 1935. Buried in Oakwood Cemetery, Tunica, Miss.

CHARLES LIVINGSTON O'NEALE

Born, Columbia, S.C., July 24, 1873, entered The Citadel, 1889, Pay Cadet, initiated 1889, Transferred to Rho.(University of South Carolina). Insurance, Merchant/Broker. He married Carolyn W. O'Neale and lived in Spartanburg, S.C. He died on October 6, 1943 and is buried at Greenlawn Memorial Cemetery in Spartanburg, S.C.

Peter Keys McCully,
Courtesy: The Citadel Archives & Museum,Charleston, SC

THETA SECOND 1890 INITIATES

ROBERT BENJAMIN GILCHRIST

Born, Charleston, S.C., February 18,1871, entered The Citadel, 1888, Pay Cadet, initiated 1890, Mason, Banker. He married Georgette Relph Holmes Gilchrist. He died on April 19, 1930 and is buried at Magnolia Cemetery, Charleston, S.C.

ROBERT MEANS McCAW PERRIN

Born, Abbeville, S.C., July 14, 1873, entered The Citadel, 1889, Beneficiary Cadet, initiated, 1890, Presbyterian, B.S. Degree, LL.B Degree, University of South Carolina Law School, 1897. Married, Jane Dubose Jones, Lawyer, Principal, New Orleans Academy. He died on September 8, 1938 and is buried at Upper Long Cane Presbyterian Cemetery, Abbeville, S.C. A window in Summerall Chapel is named in his honor.

Knights of the Order

THETA SECOND INITIATES 1920-1924

There were a total of 19 men initiated in the 1920-1924 time period. The year and number initiated are as follows:

1920	10
1921	6
1922	1
1923	0
1924	<u>2</u>
Total	19

Knights of the Order

THETA SECOND 1920 INITIATES

JULIUS BLAKE MIDDLETON

Born, Charleston, S.C., November 9, 1900, entered The Citadel, 1916, Pay Cadet, initiated into Kappa Alpha Order by Beta Gamma, May 6, 1920, Badge # 4649, Mason, B.S. degree. He was employed in Ohio as a Petroleum Technologist. He married Margaret Lane Goodwyn Middleton (1904-1998), daughter of former Citadel Commandant (1923-1926), Colonel Albert Gallatin Goodwyn, a grandson of President John Tyler. He and his wife later lived in Summerville, S.C. and he died in April, 1986. He is buried in the churchyard of St. Philip's Church, Charleston, S.C.

WILLIAM ALBERT DOTTERER

Born, Charleston, S.C., August 8, 1999, entered The Citadel, 1917, Pay Cadet, initiated into Kappa Alpha Order by Beta Gamma, May 7, 1920, Badge # 4647, Resigned from The Citadel June 9, 1920. Episcopal, Mason. He married Mary Sue Bolt. He was a realtor with Stevenson, Zimmerman & Company in Charleston. He was a member of St. Philip's Church. He died on February 11, 1968 and is buried at St. Philip's Church, Charleston, S.C.

HUGH McCUTCHEON JAMES

Born, Wilson's Mill, S.C., August 25, 1899, entered The Citadel, 1916, Pay Cadet, initiated into Kappa Alpha Order by Beta Gamma, May 7, 1920, Badge #4648, Episcopal, B.S. degree. He married Clara

Hugh McCutcheon James,
Courtesy: The Citadel Archives & Museum,Charleston, SC

Knights of the Order

Tillman James. He worked as a sales manager in Jacksonville, FL for many years. He died on November 6, 1969 of a heart attack while on vacation with his wife in Bangkok, Thailand. He is buried at Elmwood Cemetery, Columbia, S.C.

ANGUS WILSON RILEY

Angus Wilson Riley

Born, Bamberg, S.C., December 8, 1899, entered The Citadel, 1916, Pay Cadet, initiated into Kappa Alpha Order by Beta Gamma, May 7, 1920, Badge # 4560. On January 18, 1922, he married Margaret Evans Edens. He was a banker at Planters National Bank. He served in the US Army during World War II. Angus Wilson Riley died on April 15, 1981 at the age of 82 and is buried in the Cave Methodist Church cemetery in Allendale, S.C.

JOHN PERRYCLEAR SCOVILLE

Born, Orangeburg, S.C., March 25, 1899, entered The Citadel, 1917, Pay Cadet, initiated into Kappa Alpha Order by Beta Gamma, May 7, 1920, Badge #4652, B.S degree. Elk, Mason. He married Annie M. Scoville. He was a Maintenance Superintendent for the South Carolina Highway Department in Barnwell, S.C. He died on April 18, 1967 and is buried at the Church of the Apostles Methodist Cemetery in Barnwell, S.C.

John Perryclear Scoville

196

EUGENE BATTLE SMITH

Born, St. Louis, Mo., May 18, 1899, entered
The Citadel, 1916, Pay Cadet, initiated into
Kappa Alpha Order by Beta Gamma, May 7,
1920, Badge # 4651. Married, Mary Smith.
He worked as a Chemist (Druggist). He died
March 20, 1970 and is buried Calvary Cem-
etery, St. Louis, Mo.

Eugene Battle Smith

LUCIAN CARY WHITAKER

Born, Charleston, S.C., April 16, 1899, entered The Citadel, 1917, Pay Cadet, initiated
into Kappa Alpha Order by Beta Gamma,
May 7, 1920, Badge # 4653. He married Lu-
cile V. Wilson on July 6, 1929. He joined the
United States Marine Corps and rose to the
rank of Lt. Colonel. During World War II,
he commanded the Camp Lejune Women's
Reserve School and the recruit depot. He
was an aide to General Smedley Butler. Lucian Cary Whitaker died on March 4, 1951
and is buried along with his wife at Arlington
National Cemetery.

Lucian Cary Whitaker

ROBERT EDWARD LEE

Born, Florence, S.C., January 12, 1901, entered
The Citadel, 1918, Pay Cadet, initiated into
Kappa Alpha Order by Beta Gamma, October
23, 1920, Badge # 5342, Baptist, B.S. degree,
Civil Engineer. Married, Mary Clinton Orr.

Robert Edward Lee

Retired as a Supervisor of Arnall Mills, Sargent, GA. Died, March 16, 1993 at age 92. He is buried at Oak Hill Cemetery, Newnan, Ga.

EVANDER ERVIN BROWN

Born, Darlington, S.C., December 11, 1900, entered The Citadel, 1918, Beneficiary Cadet, initiated into Kappa Alpha Order by Beta Gamma, June 11, 1920, Badge # 4681. Found Deficient in Academics in Official Registry, 1919-1920 and left school after two years. He listed his occupation as a Rate Agent in the 1940 Census. He married Elizabeth F. Barnes in 1930. He died on April 29, 1960 and is buried at Grove Hill Cemetery, Darlington, S.C.

LOUIS SEEL POULNOT

Born, Charleston, S.C., July 28, 1901, entered The Citadel, 1918, Pay Cadet, initiated into Kappa Alpha Order by Beta Gamma, June 11, 1920, Badge # 4680. He married Madelyn Maull Roberts. He operated a dry goods store in Charleston. He served in the U.S. Navy in World War II. He died on July 7, 1980 and is buried at Magnolia Cemetery in Charleston, S.C.

THETA SECOND 1921 INITIATES

WILLIAM OSCAR BRICE

Born, Columbia, S.C., December 10, 1898, entered The Citadel, 1917, Beneficiary Cadet, initiated into Kappa Alpha Order by Beta Gamma, March 3, 1921, Badge # 5293. Prior to attending The Citadel, joined the U.S. Army and served in World War I. He married Rebekah Jennings. After graduating from The Citadel in 1921, William Oscar Brice became a career Marine aviation officer. During World War II, he commanded units at every level of marine aviation. After the war, he was Director of Marine Aviation. He rose to the four star rank of full General. His last command was Commanding General, Fleet Marine Force, Pacific. General Brice died on January 30, 1972 and is buried at Zion Presbyterian Cemetery, Winnsboro, S.C.

William Oscar Brice

JOHN LAWRENCE GRAMLING

Born, Orangeburg, S.C., October 14, 1900, entered The Citadel, 1918, Pay Cadet, initiated into Kappa Alpha Order by Beta Gamma. March 4, 1921, Badge # 5292, Found Deficient in Academics in 1919-1920, 1920-1921, 1921-1922. Methodist, C.E. degree, Farmer. Married, Virginia Farnum Gramling. Died December 12, 1970, buried at Memorial Park Cemetery, Orangeburg, S.C. His son, Johnny Gramling was a famous quarterback at the University of South Carolina in the 1950's.

Knights of the Order

JAMES LEE PLATT

Born, Mullins, S.C, October 6, 1900, entered The Citadel, 1917, Beneficiary Cadet,
initiated into Kappa Alpha Order by Beta
Gamma, March 4, 1921, Badge #5290,
transferred to Alpha Nu chapter at George
Washington University. Methodist. B.S degree from The Citadel, and a Juris Doctor
degree from George Washington University. He practiced law in Mullins and King-
stree, SC. He was also the owner and editor

James Lee Platt

of the *Mullins Enterprise* and *Myrtle Beach News*. He was Past President
of the Association of Weekly Newspapers of South Carolina. He
died on December 17, 1973 and is buried at Cedardale Cemetery in
Mullins, S.C.

THOMAS QUARLES McGEE

Born, Spartanburg, S.C., June 5, 1902,
entered The Citadel, 1918, Pay Cadet,
initiated into Kappa Alpha Order by Beta
Gamma, May 20, 1921, Badge # 5343,
Presbyterian, B.S. degree. He married
Kathleen Newby McGee. He was a Paul
Harris Fellow in the Rotary Club. McGee
was President of the August W. Smith Co.
in Spartanburg, SC. He died in Spartanburg, S.C. on November 24, 1968 and is
buried in Oakwood Cemetery.

Thomas Quarles McGee

BENJAMIN A. MUNNERLYN II

Born, Columbia, S.C., September 6, 1901, entered The Citadel, 1918, Pay Cadet, initiated into Kappa Alpha Order by Beta Gamma, May 22, 1921, Badge # 5344. Honorably Discharged, February 20, 1920, returned, Honorably Discharged again, June 10, 1921. Episcopal, Married Margaret S. Munnerlyn. He moved to Jacksonville, FL where he worked the rest of his life. He was a Steamship Agent

Benjamin A. Munnerlyn II

for most of his life, and later was the Secretary-Treasurer of Builders Supply Co. at the time of his death. He was a member of St. Marks Episcopal Church and The Florida Yacht Club. He died on September 15, 1952 and is buried at Evergreen Cemetery, Jacksonville, Fla.

ORLANDO CLARENDON MOOD

Born, Summerton, S.C., December 1, 1899, entered The Citadel, 1917, Pay Cadet, initiated into Kappa Alpha Order by Beta Gamma, May 22, 1921, Badge #5350, Methodist, Mason, B.S. degree. He married Mildred Mood. He was a career Army officer, serving at Ft. Benning, Ga. in the 1930's. He was the Assistant Chief of staff for Supply during the invasion of North Africa in November, 1942. On September 22, 1943, as a full Colonel, he

Orlando Clarendon Mood

was awarded the Legion of Merit for his work on that operation. He was promoted to Brigadier General on June 12, 1945 and awarded

the Distinguished Service Medal. As a Major General in 1953, he was given a second award of the Distinguished Service Medal. General Mood died on May 2, 1953, and he and his wife are buried at Arlington National Cemetery.

THETA SECOND 1922 INITIATES

FRANCIS BONNEAU CARSON

Born, Spartanburg, S.C., July 27, 1901, entered The Citadel, 1921, Pay Cadet, initiated into Kappa Alpha Order by Beta Gamma, April 19, 1922, Badge # 5588. Resigned from The Citadel, March 13, 1922. His father, Ralph Kennedy Carson, was a prominent attorney and his mother, Catherine Johnson Carson, donated the portrait of Joel Poinsett that hangs in the Charleston Museum. He died on April 12, 1978 at age 77 and is buried at the Church of the Advent (Episcopal) in Spartanburg, S.C.

Knights of the Order

THETA SECOND 1924 INITIATES

EUGENE WILLIAMS BLACK

Born, Walterboro, S.C., January 11, 1900, entered The Citadel, 1919, Pay Cadet, initiated into Kappa Alpha Order by Beta Gamma, March 3, 1924, Badge # 5291, Episcopal, B.S. Mason, K.P. Married Nancey Wells Black. Died in Walterboro, SC on June 18, 1937 at age 37 and is buried at Live Oak Cemetery, Walterboro, S.C.

MARLBOROUGH PEGUES

Born, Pelzer, S.C., February 5, 1904, entered The Citadel, 1920, Pay Cadet, initiated into Kappa Alpha Order by Beta Gamma, April 9, 1924, Badge #6719, Episcopal, B.S degree. He married Susalee Belser of Columbia, SC on November 22, 1944. Cadet Pegues played football for the Citadel and was known by his nickname of "Mollie". District Manager for Standard Oil Company in Charleston, S.C. Seventeen days after his marriage, he was accidentally shot while deer hunting and died on December 9, 1944 at age 41. He is buried in the Christ Episcopal Church cemetery in Greenville, S.C.

Marlborough Pegues

Knights of the Order

MEMORIABILIA

Knights of the Order

JULIUS BLAKE MIDDLETON

Charleston, S. C.

✦

"Blake"—"Goat"—"Daddy Rabbit"

✦

Chemistry

"Mine honor is my life; both grow in one;
Take honor from me, and my life is done."
Shakespeare

Private Company "C" (4); Corporal Company
"A" (4); Sergeant Company "A", First Sergeant
Company "B" (2); Captain Company "D", Private
Company "D", First Lieutenant Company "A" (1);
Librarian Y. M. C. A. (4), Secretary (3); Regular
Corps Honor Committee (4, 3, 2, 1), Secretary
(1); Member Citadel Triangular Debating Team
(2); Senior Hop Committee (4); Thanksgiving Hop
Committee (3), Chairman Senior Committee, Christ-
mas Hop Committee (2); Official Hop Committee
(2); Assistant Football Manager (2), Manager (1);
Swimming Team (4, 3, 2); Member Charleston Club
(4, 3, 2, 1), Secretary (2); Rifle Team Regular
(2, 1).

✦

AS may be observed above, the most outstanding cognomen by which this good-looking
young fellow is known at the old Citadel
is "Daddy." And how well he merits his
nickname! Blake hasn't been known to rush many
of the fair damsels during his career here, but with
those on whom he has lavished his attentions he
has always been "Daddy Rabbit." In his own
words: "What's the use of going with a girl if
you don't stand in well enough with her to put
all other amorous clamorers 'on the rocks'?"
But Blake's little "affaires d'amour" haven't prevented his fine qualities from coming to the fore.
His military ability was recognized in his junior
year when he was promoted to a First Sergeantcy.
And his Senior year found him with nothing less
than Captain's chevrons on his sleeve. This didn't
turn his head, tho, for he continued to be the
"good fellow" that he had been previously. Blake
has no enemies. Everyone who meets him is in-
stantly captivated with his winning smile, charming
personality, and gentlemanly manners. That he has
many friends is evidenced by his having been
elected Football Manager in his Senior year. It
may also be added here that he was Chairman of
the Senior Hop Committee in his Junior year, and
has served on several other important hop committees. Lastly, the valuation which former Classes
have attached to Blake's character has been demonstrated by the fact that in every one of his four
years here he has been elected to serve on the
finest possession of The Citadel, the Corps Honor
Committee.
All of your classmates wish you luck, Blake.
May you be as successful in life as you have been
within the walls of the S. C. M. C.

Appendix - Memoriabilia

1917-18 — Private Co. B;
Prize Company; R. O.
T. C., Plattsburg, N. Y.;
Substitute Honor Com-
mittee.

1918-19 — Private Co. B;
Corporal Co. B; Xmas
Hop Committee; S. A.
T. C.

1919-20 — Private Co. B;
Thanksgiving and Senior
Hop Committees; Ameri-
can Legion; Assistant
Standing Hop Commit-
tee.

1920-21 — Private Co. B;
Manager Football Team;
Chairman Standing Hop
Committee.

HUGH McCUTCHEON JAMES
"Jesse"

Summerton, S. C.

Physics, Elective, B.S

He who has been at it longest, knows better the rules of the game. The man referred to is no other than "JESSE" JAMES. He is the veritable lion of the Citadel social world—many a heart has beat faster when "HUGH" approached to claim a dance—and there are others—but ask "AL,"—he knows. "JESSE" has held positions on the various hop committees during his "term" at The Citadel, and now, as chairman of the official hop committee, has proved worthy of the honor thrust upon him—and the many enjoyable dances were due to this boy.

The BLUE AND WHITE owes a lot to Jesse, who has done his part—whether on the field helping to make stronger varsity, or on the side lines rooting for a Bull-dog victory. He was in part re-warded in being elected football manager, and the team enjoyed the best schedule they have ever had.

He is a good student and is well-liked by every member of the faculty. Always obliging, big-hearted, generous and friendly, this boy has won a host of friends.

Our school days are over—we must say good-bye and move on—and we say good-bye to "JESSE" with the best wishes for every success in anything he may undertake.

ANGUS WILSON RILEY
Allendale, S. C.

✛

"Ang"

✛

Physics

"Or light or dark, or short or tall,
He sets his springe to snare them all."

Private Company "C" (4); Private Company "C" (3); Private Company "C", Sergeant Company "C" (2); Lieutenant Company "A", Private Company "A" (1); Christmas Hop Committee (4); Thanksgiving Hop Committee (3); Senior Hop Committee (2); Chairman Official Hop Committee (1); Prize Company (4, 3).

✛

LO, the apple of milady's eye approacheth! Gentle reader, behold **Angus**, the dashing Beau Brummel, whose good looks and winning ways are exceeded only by his fondness for the fair sex and their only too willing reciprocation of his sentiment.

Yes, you have guessed it—**"Ang"** is a "ladies' man." Himself possessing a very comely countenance, he is only too quick to recognize such qualities among our dear friends, the ladies, and, altho struggling manfully to distribute his favors with impartiality, an exceptionally pretty face will sometimes cause him to give its owner more than a passing glance; and a broken heart is the result.

Never has there been a "Rat" who has created such a furor among the Charleston lassies as did this boy, and ever since their form of greeting has been, "Hello ————! How's **Angus?**" As a dancer, he is in a class by himself, being a past master of the art, and some day bids fair to rival Terpsichore herself. We hope, gentle reader, that you are not getting a false impression, and picturing **Angus** as a Bluebeard, a male vampire, or what not. That would be an unpardonable sin on our part. In a word, he is the prince of good fellows, and holds one of the highest places in the opinion of the Cadets.

Angus chose Physics as his elective. Why? We don't know, unless it was to discover the whys and wherefores of his "magnetic" personality.

Altho his aspirations in the military line have never risen to any great height, his merit was nevertheless recognized by the Commandant, who conferred upon him the rank of Second Lieutenant.

"Bunny," old boy, it has indeed been a pleasure to have known you, to say nothing of the privilege of having had you as a classmate, and, altho it is with regret that we bid you "good bye," we know that, when you have left the protecting walls of your alma mater, nothing but success awaits you in the years to come.

210

1917-18 — Private Co. D;
Football Team; Baseball
Team.

1918-19 — Private Co. D;
Thanksgiving Hop Com-
mittee; Varsity Baseball.

1919-20 — Private Co. D;
Christmas Hop Commit-
tee; Football Team;
Varsity Baseball.

1920-21 — Private Co. D;
Football Team; Thanks-
giving Hop Committee;
Baseball Team.

JOHN PERRYCLEAR SCOVILLE
"Johnnie," "Shag"
Orangeburg, S. C.
Physics, Elective, B.S

" . . . . . and some have greatness thrust upon them!" Great in heart; a great football player; a great baseball player; and, a great old friend. We present to you "JOHNNIE" SCOVILLE who, by his generosity, friendliness, and consideration of everyone, from the highest ranking officer to the lowliest "rat," has endeared himself to all his fellow cadets.

"JOHNNIE" from the first day of his arrival at Citadel for early football practice was destined for prominence in athletics; for during his four years at The Citadel, he has won three block C's on the gridiron, and four ovals on the baseball diamond. "SHAG'S" football career is history with the cadets, for it was he who scored the winning touchdown in our annual fray with Carolina in '19. His diminu-tive stature has not in any way been a detriment to his playing. The grit, determination, and fight that characterize a Citadel team are all combined in "LITTLE JOHNNIE."

As he is prominent in the athletic world, likewise he is prominent in the social life at Citadel. Many are the hop committees that he has served on, and his name on any committee is an assurance of the success of any dance. With his ability as a dancer and with his "gift o' gab," few are the ladies that can resist his *sweet nothings*.

SCOVILLE has, in the military game, achieved that which is the envy of all cadets—Senior Privates. For four years he has "soljered" with "D" Company, and always with a clean sleeve. "SHAG'S" work in the classroom has always been excellent. As a physicist he is inferior to none—save "Fuzzy."

Now we bid farewell to one of the best "scouts" we have ever known. "JOHNNIE," if in your scramble with the word you are able to take hard knocks and come up again smiling, as you have done time and time again on the football field, without a doubt you will reach your goal in life, whate're it may be.

Knights of the Order

EUGENE BATTLE SMITH
St. Louis, Mo.

✛

"Ludendorff"—"Battle"

✛

Chemistry—Biology

"His grandeur he derived from heaven alone,
For he was great ere fortune made him so."

Private Company "C" (4); Corporal Company "C" (3); First Sergeant Company "A" (2); Captain Company "A" (1); Rifle Team; National Rifle Matches, Camp Perry, Ohio, 1918; National Rifle Matches, Caldwell, N. J., 1919; Swimming Team (1, 3, 2, 1), Manager (1); Plattsburg R. O. T. C. Camp, 1918; Camp Lee, Virginia, 1919; Vice-President Senior Class (1); Honor Committee (3).

✛

ET'S get an apple." How's that? Oh! of course you realize who it is that speaks, "Battle," our stalwart Missouri classmate, arrives on the scene.

Is he a physical culturist? No, we can't say that, for he has been known to frequent the "Lab" under John D.'s guidance more than once.

Altho being a regular athletic devil, "Battle" had a certain wild experience during the past which has kept him from invading the football world, much to our regret as well as his despair. But has this dismayed him? Ah! No! Far be it from him; for he is a king in the social world.

However, he is only **one** lady's man, dismaying many and encouraging few, we find his whole social life centered in the one girl who lives—am I right when I say it?—near Ye Olde Colonial Lake.

Yet, reader, I am digressing from the true character which is our hero's, for he is our leader and counsellor in the military affairs of the College. To him we take our military grievances and injuries, for which he gives ready advice and real sympathy. We find in him a real true-hearted and unprejudiced leader, upholding the ideals and precedents of his alma mater, handed down to him thru the files of Senior Captains.

Thinking first of the Corps and its envied standing in the military world, his one great ideal has been to raise it still higher, leaving no power of his unused to keep our position, as it has been, one of honor and credit to the "wearers of the Gray."

But, reader, have you noticed anything particular about his picture? Behold the handsomest man in the Battalion! He is the unchallenged owner of that distinction. I know you will agree with me on this subject; yet there is more to "Battle" than the insert can tell, for, bearing a personality that is catching, he holds the highest esteem and admiration of his fellow-Cadets.

It is to you, its leader, "Battle," that the Corps extends its fondest farewell, and wishes for you even greater success in life than that which has attended you during your stay at The Citadel.

212

Appendix - Memoriabilia

1917-18 — Private Co. A; Football Team; Track Team; Basketball Team; Baseball Team.

1918-19 — Corporal Co. B; Football Team; Track Team; Baseball Team; Thanksgiving Hop Committee; Official Hop Committee.

1919-20 — Sergeant Co. D; Football Team; Track Team; Baseball Squad; Official Hop Committee.

1920-21 — Lieutenant Co. D; Football Team; Track Team; Baseball Team; Chairman Commencement Hop Committee.

LUCIAN CAREY WHITAKER, JR.
"Cotch-um," "Lucian"
Charleston, S. C.
English-History, B.S.

A real man, a man among men, aptly characterizes this big-hearted, generous, friendly lad who is affectionately known to his fellow cadets as "COTCH-UM." By the above, one would imagine that "LUCIAN" is not at all susceptible to the charms of the fair sex; but he is a man's man, so is he also a great favorite with the ladies. In fact, no phase of cadet life would be complete without the presence of "WHITAKER."

As an athlete, it is enough to say that he is the only man of our class who wears four Block "C's," representing his ability in football, basketball, baseball, and track. From his "rat" year he has been a mainstay on all the athletic teams; playing the game in true Bulldog fashion.

In the military life, "COTCH-UM" has played the game fairly and squarely, and we find him in his senior year as a lieutenant of Company "D." "WHITAKER'S" popularity as an officer is unequalled, and this is shown by the loyalty of those whom he leads.

With all his loyalty in cadet activities, "LUCIAN" has always stood well-up in his class work, and has never forgotten why he was sent to college.

"LUCIEN," you have been a friend such as only a few can be, and in leaving the "old school," you leave a vacant place which will be hard to fill. Knowing you as we do, we realize that by your loyalty to your friends and your trueness of character, we are leaving the best "old pal" we have ever known, and if in your battle with life you conduct yourself as you have while with us, nothing but the greatest success awaits you.

"*And those who paint him best, praise him most.*"

✦

ENGINEERING

✦

From his first year at the Citadel, Bob has made friends and been a true Citadel man, indulging in all the activities of cadet life, and finding success in its every phase. He has shown himself to possess the sterling qualities of a good student and a fine gentleman.

We are forced to pass over the space allotted to military titles, knowing as we do that despite his latent ability, he has much preferred the easy life of a private, rather than the responsibilities of rank.

In both social and athletic fields, "Bob" has met with high honors. Socially he is conceded to be a brilliant and interesting conversationalist and a smooth and popular dancer, besides serving on numerous hop committees. In athletics he has starred four years on the football team, and so earned the distinctive honor of captain his final year. He shall be sorely missed and more than hard to replace.

We, his classmates, bid him "Good Luck and Happy Days," while we watch him pass through the sallyport to play the game of life with the same high ideals and upright principles of manhood and character that he used here, to endear him so to us.

ROBERT EDWARD LEE
MARION, S. C.

1919-20—Pvt., Co. "B"; Pee Dee Club; Varsity Football; Senior Hop Comm. 1920-21— Pvt., Co. "B"; Hazing Comm.; Varsity Football. 1922-23—Pvt., Co. "B"; Varsity Football; Chrmn., Senior Hop Comm. Comm. Hop. Comm. 1923-24— 2nd Lt., Co. "D"; Pvt., Co. "D"; Varsity Football; Capt., Football; S. P. P. C. Club.

"BOB"

1924

THE SPHINX

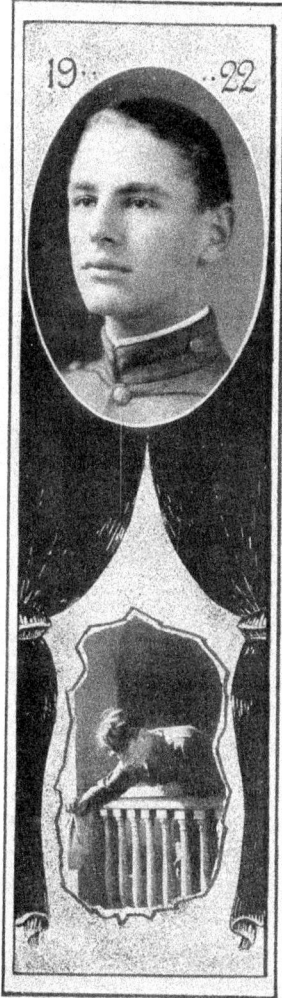

LOUIS SEEL POULNOT

Charleston, S. C.

"Louis"

Engineering—B. S.

"Good nature and good sense could ever join."

1918-19— Private Company "A"; Charleston Club.

1919-20—Corporal Company "A"; Private Company "A"; Artillery Club; Charleston Club.

1920-21—Private Company "A"; Band; Charleston Club; Artillery Club; Fort Monroe.

1921-22—Private Company "A"; Charleston Club; Thanksgiving Hop Committee; Ten-Inch Club; Member S. P. P. C.; Calliopean Literary Society.

One bright September morning, about four years ago, **Louis Seel Poulnot** entered the sallyport of this old school. He was one of the several cadets-to-be who hailed from the renowned "City by the Sea."

Poulnot completed his "rat" year with such a creditable showing that he became a corporal; but he did this merely to show what he could do. His Junior year found him in surroundings not conducive to the making of a Senior Captain, so he gave up the glory of the golden chevrons, and now, in his Senior year, we find him a member of that well-known, time-honored band of good fellows—the S. P. P. C.

In the academic department, "**Louis**" has always stood among the first, and the ease with which he has obtained this standing is a clear indication of his powerful mind. His athletic activities have been confined mostly to the side lines, where he has helped to win many a contest by his lusty cheering. He is a strong supporter of every Citadel activity.

"**Louis**" is a good mixer, and when he so desires makes quite a hit with the fair and aristocratic ladies of Charleston. He has early proved a leader in the social life of **The Citadel**, and there is not a single well-informed "Miss" in the city who does not know of this attractive young fellow. There is no social function complete when he is missing; and many are the hearts that are gladdened when he is near.

Poulnot is a true, honorable, and lovable cadet, and to part with him will be one of the biggest trials of his Class, and of the entire Corps.

Luck to you, "**Louis**"; you deserve it. The best friends must part, and it is with regret that we say, "Good-bye."

1922

215

Knights of the Order

1917-18 — Private Co. A.

1918-19 — Corporal Co. A; Prize Company; Second Lieutenant. U. S. A.; Shavetail Club; Senior Hop Committee.

1919-20—First Sergeant Co. D; American Legion; Vice-Post Commander; Polytechnic Literary Society; Vice-President Intercollegiate Oratorical Association;

1919-20 —Continued. Honor Committee; Senior Hop Committee; Christmas Hop Committee.

1920-21 — Captain Co. D; Post Commander American Legion; Polytechnic Literary Society; President South Carolina Inter-collegiate Association; Honor Committee Secretary; Cheer Leader; Standing Hop Committee; Hazing Committee.

WILLIAM OSCAR BRICE
"Oscar," "Irish"

Winnesboro, S. C.

English-History, B.S.

"Aw right, fellows! Blue and White!" . . . and then you see OSCAR in action, and having seen him, you will agree that few cheer leaders equal and none surpass the man who for the past two years has led the corps in every athletic event in which the BULLDOG team has taken part. Brice has not taken part as an athlete in athletics, but to say that he has taken no part in athletics would be wrong, for no one man has done more to bring about victory for the BLUE AND WHITE than has OSCAR, whose PEP never diminishes, and who is by far the hardest fighter on or off the field.

It was in the summer of 1918 that WILLIAM O. BRICE decided "that it wasn't playing the game, so he slammed his books away," and answered the call of the colors. He won his commission in the U. S. infantry at the training camp at Plattsburg and served as a lieutenant until the armistice was signed. He returned to THE CITADEL, and it was then that we realized that a real military genius had come into our midst. He began by instructing us in the new method of bayonet fighting, and all credit is due him for the efficiency of the battalion in that respect. After having served his year as First Sergeant, Company D, he now holds the position as Captain of that organization, a leader in every sense of the word.

OSCAR is as popular with the ladies as he is with the cadets. This cannot be attributed to his good looks, so it must be on account of his striking personality and genial disposition, which no one is able to resist.

We predict for OSCAR a career in the army, but wherever he goes he has the best wishes of every man in the corps.

Appendix - Memoriabilia

1917-18 — Private Co. A;
Polytechnic Literary So-
ciety; Varsity Football;
R. O. T. C., Plattsburg,
N. Y.

1918-19 — Corporal Co. A;
Polytechnic Literary So-
ciety.

1919-20 — Sergeant Co. B;
Sergeant Co. A; Poly-
technic Literary Society;
Assistant Editor-in-Chief
"Sphinx, '20"; Y. M.
C. A.

1920-21 — Lieutenant Co. B;
President Polytechnic
Literary Society; Edi-
tor - in - Chief "Sphinx,
'21"; Y. M. C. A.

JAMES LEE PLATT, JR.
"Jim"
Mullins, S. C.
English-Biology, B.S.

In every group of men there is always one who takes the lead, whether in athletics, military, society, scholarship, or what not, and "JIM" PLATT is one of these. Through three years' association with him, it is clearly illustrated to his classmates that he was the man who would take up the great task of being Editor-in-Chief of the "SPHINX, '21," and behold, kind reader, both the man and his work.

In his freshman year "JIM" took an active part in athletics, winning his letter in football, but since then his activity in Citadel life has been confined to literary circles, in which he excels.

At the end of his freshman year "PLATT" was rewarded for his hard work on the drill field by being appointed to attend the R. O. T. C. camp at Plattsburg, N. Y., and upon returning to The Citadel in September he was, like Napoleon, made a corporal and again assigned to Company A. Since then the chevrons have never left his sleeves; rising from corporal to a sergeant in his junior year, and graduating as "Lieutenant Co. B, sir."

He did not answer the call of the "wild" (social world) until in his junior year, and since that time he has taken an active part in all things pertaining to social functions. His good looks and manly physique have attracted many a glance from the fair ones.

"JIMMIE," we have learned during the past four years, not only to love and respect you as a class-mate, but as a man of personality, ability, honor, and all those traits which tend, when combined, to form the ideal man. We leave you, old fellow, and will watch with interest the glorious career which is sure to be yours in the future.

217

TOM QUARLES McGEE
Spartanburg, S. C.

"Tom" "Above our life, we love a true friend." "Thomas"

1919-20—Private Company "C"; Camp Lee; Swimming Team; Piedmont Club.
1920-21—Corporal Company "C"; Spartanburg Club; Swimming Team; The Five Club; Prize Company.
1921-22—Quartermaster Sergeant Company "C"; Hastoc Club; Standing Hop Committee; Spartanburg Club; Camp McClellan.
1922-23—First Lieutenant Company "C"; President Spartanburg Club; Hastoc Club; Varsity Basketball Squad.

"Tom" joined our class in our Sophomore year, leaving the Class of '22 to become a member of the Class of '23. Even with the handicap of this late start "Tom" soon made a place in the class that can be filled by no one else. His gentlemanliness, friendliness and loyalty have given "Tom" popularity that any one might envy.

In the military line, "Tom" has experienced a continual rising success. His ability on the drill field is undisputed and has given him the rank of First Lieutenant.

Among the ladies, "Thomas" is just "Tom," and one might think that this lad would have fallen a victim to some of their fair charms, but it seems as though there is some one "back home."

"Tom" has not made a record as an athlete, but he has been there trying wherever there was need for men.

In conclusion, let us say that the squareness and "trueblueness" "TOM" has shown cannot help but gain for him a large share of that elusive phantom called Success.

I SHOULD HAVE FINESSED—

1923

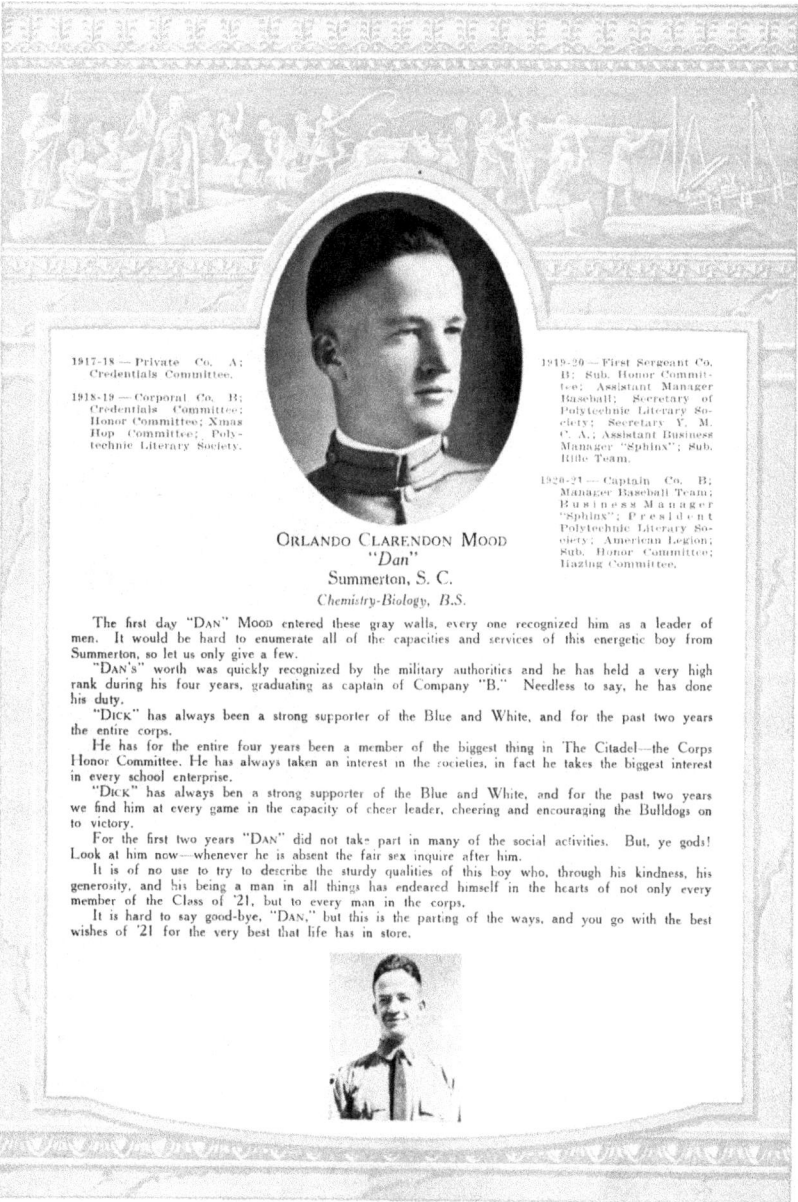

1917-18 — Private Co. A; Credentials Committee.

1918-19 — Corporal Co. B; Credentials Committee; Honor Committee; Xmas Hop Committee; Polytechnic Literary Society.

1919-20 — First Sergeant Co. B; Sub. Honor Committee; Assistant Manager Baseball; Secretary of Polytechnic Literary Society; Secretary Y. M. C. A.; Assistant Business Manager "Sphinx"; Sub. Rifle Team.

1920-21 — Captain Co. B; Manager Baseball Team; Business Manager "Sphinx"; President Polytechnic Literary Society; American Legion; Sub. Honor Committee; Hazing Committee.

ORLANDO CLARENDON MOOD
"Dan"
Summerton, S. C.
Chemistry-Biology, B.S.

The first day "DAN" MOOD entered these gray walls, every one recognized him as a leader of men. It would be hard to enumerate all of the capacities and services of this energetic boy from Summerton, so let us only give a few.

"DAN'S" worth was quickly recognized by the military authorities and he has held a very high rank during his four years, graduating as captain of Company "B." Needless to say, he has done his duty.

"DICK" has always been a strong supporter of the Blue and White, and for the past two years the entire corps.

He has for the entire four years been a member of the biggest thing in The Citadel—the Corps Honor Committee. He has always taken an interest in the societies, in fact he takes the biggest interest in every school enterprise.

"DICK" has always ben a strong supporter of the Blue and White, and for the past two years we find him at every game in the capacity of cheer leader, cheering and encouraging the Bulldogs on to victory.

For the first two years "DAN" did not take part in many of the social activities. But, ye gods! Look at him now—whenever he is absent the fair sex inquire after him.

It is of no use to try to describe the sturdy qualities of this boy who, through his kindness, his generosity, and his being a man in all things has endeared himself in the hearts of not only every member of the Class of '21, but to every man in the corps.

It is hard to say good-bye, "DAN," but this is the parting of the ways, and you go with the best wishes of '21 for the very best that life has in store.

Knights of the Order

EUGENE WILLIAMS BLACK
Walterboro, S. C.

"Gene"

English and History—B. S.

"Forbade to wade through slaughter to a throne,
And shut the gates of mercy on mankind."

1918-19 Private Company "B"; Rifle Team, Caldwell, N. J.

1919-20 Corporal Company "C"; Rifle Team, Camp Perry, Ohio.

1920-21 Sergeant-Major, "Staff"; Expert Rifleman; Camp Knox Club.

1921-22 Lieutenant and Adjutant "Staff"; Lieutenant Company "A"; Chairman Thanksgiving Hop.

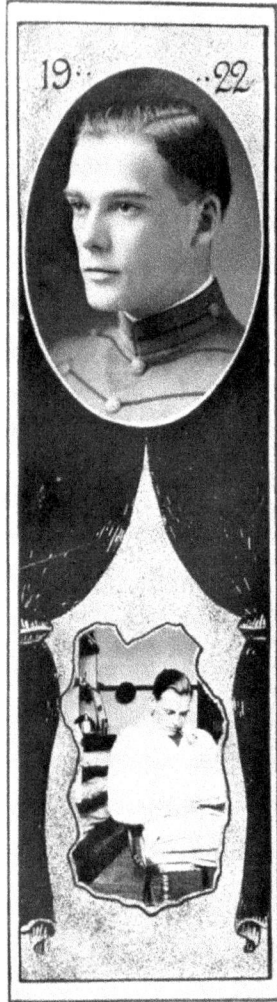

Many small towns produce great men, and Walterboro is no exception to this rule. "Gene's" greatness lies in his ability to mix with any crowd. He is easily one of the most popular officers at this institution—a position which he holds by his own ability, and not because of any "pull." He is one officer who stands on his own merits, and does not seek to climb the ladder of success at the expense of his fellow-Cadets or the filling of the demerit book, and yet who can say that he has never shirked any duty.

At first, "Gene" had little or no social aspirations, but at the beginning of his Sophomore year he entered the social world, where his winning smile and general good fellowship won for him the admiration of the "ladies" as well as that of the Corps.

"Gene" has never been known as an athlete, but there has never been a more loyal supporter of Citadel athletics; and never a game of any kind is played but that "Gene" is on the sidelines rooting hard for his "Alma Mater."

From the very first, "Gene" showed his ability to handle a rifle, and has been a member of every rifle team that has represented The Citadel for the last four years; and for the success of these teams "Gene" has been greatly responsible. He was a member of the teams that went to Caldwell and Perry.

There are some men who are capable of holding the good will of a large body of men indefinitely, and such is "Gene". When the farewells have been said, and the Class of 1922 is disbanded and scattered over the land, there is not one but that will remember this manly, big-hearted, generous fellow. "Gene", old fellow, the chain of friendship that you have forged between our class and yourself will not be broken, though we be scattered to the four corners of the earth.

19 22

220

MARLBOROUGH PEGUES
GREENVILLE, S. C.

1920-21 — Pvt., Co. "A";
Swimming Team; Basketball
Squad; Piedmont Club. 1921-22
Pvt., Co. "B"; Cpl., Co. "B";
Pvt., Co. "B"; Prize Company;
Swimming Team; Basketball
Squad; Sub., Rifle Team. 1922-
23—Pvt., Co. "B"; Sgt., Co.
"B"; Pvt., Co. "B"; Swimming
Team; Basketball Squad; Mgr.,
Freshman Football Team; R.
O. T. C. Camp, Ft. Monroe,
Va. 1923-24—2nd Lt., Co. "A";
Pvt., Co. "A"; Capt. and Mgr.,
Swimming Team; Varsity Foot-
ball; S. P. P. C. Club; Thanks-
giving Hop Comm.; Com. Hop
Comm; Asso. Ed., The Sphinx.

"MOLLY"

1924

*"Light or dark, short or tall, he sets
his snares to catch them all."*

✛

CHEMISTRY

✛

"MOLLY'S" success was pronounced almost coincident with his passage through
the sallyport of the Old Citadel. As a
Freshman, he won the friendship of every
member of the corps by his winning personality.

"MOLLY" never did agree with the military authorities, and on account of de-
merits could not hold the high positions
which were thrust upon him from time to
time. He is now numbered among the
S. P. P. C.'s.

Socially, "MOLLY" is a complete success
which is well proven by the number of hop
committees on which he has served, and
being unanimously chosen as the best dancer in the corps.

For four years "MOLLY" has been one of
the most valuable men on the basketball
and swimming teams, being elected captain of the swimming team in his Senior
year. Unfortunately he did not try football until his Senior year when he made
his letter. His record in football this year
is one which we can hardly forget.

"MOLLY," we wish you the same success
in the future as you have had for the four
years that we have known you.

Knights of the Order

March, 1944

University of Pennsylvania
Law Review
And American Law Register
FOUNDED 1852

Copyright 1944, by the University of Pennsylvania.

| VOL. 92 | MARCH, 1944 | No. 3 |

WILLIAM EPHRAIM MIKELL

EDWIN R. KEEDY †

William Ephraim Mikell, who taught in this Law School for forty-six years, died in Charleston, South Carolina, on January 20th and was buried on Edisto Island, where his ancestors settled nearly two and one-half centuries ago.

He was born January 29, 1868, in Sumter, South Carolina, where he received his early education. In 1886 he won a state-wide competition for a scholarship in the South Carolina Military College, generally known as The Citadel, and four years later received the degree of Bachelor of Science from that institution. After graduating he was principal of Blackstock Academy in South Carolina for two years and then became principal of the Piedmont Seminary in Lincolnton, North Carolina. While holding this position he read Blackstone's Commentaries in the evenings and during the summer of 1894 he attended the University of Virginia Law School, of which Judge Minor was then dean, for a term of six weeks. During his stay in Lincolnton he married Miss Martha Turner McBee, who survives him. He was admitted to the Bars of North and South Carolina in 1896 and practiced several months in his birthplace, Sumter, South Carolina. The turning point in his career occurred in the spring of 1896 when he came to Philadelphia as one of the many young lawyers who were assisting George Wharton Pepper and William Draper Lewis in the preparation of the *Pepper and Lewis Digest of Pennsylvania Decisions.* In the fall of that year Dr. Lewis became Dean of the Law School and on his recommendation Mikell was appointed an instructor. His progress was rapid and he was promoted to Assistant Professor in

---

† Dean, University of Pennsylvania Law School.

(229)

This content downloaded on Tue, 15 Jan 2013 12:51:23 PM
All use subject to JSTOR Terms and Conditions

Portrait by *Alice Kent Stoddard*

WILLIAM EPHRAIM MIKELL

Knights of the Order

1899 and to Professor in 1902. When Dr. Lewis resigned the deanship in 1914, Mikell was appointed to succeed him, serving until 1929, when he retired in order to devote all his time to teaching and writing. He was made Professor Emeritus in 1938, but continued his teaching under special appointment as lecturer until the spring of 1943. After a summer spent as usual in Castine, Maine, he returned to Philadelphia and occupied an office in the Law School, where he spent his time in study and writing until the early part of January when he went to Charleston in order to escape the rigors of the northern climate.

Mikell won distinction as a teacher, scholar and administrator. Above all he was an inspiring and effective teacher. Although his formal legal education consisted of attendance for only six weeks at a lecture course, he quickly adapted himself to the case method and employed it with pronounced success. He was particularly adept in training new students to analyze and solve legal problems. He was never dogmatic, but always stimulating and suggestive. One of his favorite methods was to lead a student adroitly along a line of fallacious reasoning until the fallacy was evident to the student as well as to the other members of the class. He took delight in teaching and this was reflected in the interest of his students, whose respect and affection he always retained. His casebooks on Criminal Law and Criminal Procedure were highly regarded and extensively used by teachers of these subjects.

His writings were chiefly concerned with the Criminal Law. In other fields he wrote a volume on *Dental Jurisprudence* and an article on the "Treaty-Making Power of the President and the Senate of the United States." He also contributed the *Life of Roger Brooke Taney* to the series, *Great American Lawyers*, and wrote several articles on the same subject. He was a member of the Editorial Committee of the Association of American Law Schools, which edited *Select Essays in Anglo-American Legal History* and the *Continental Legal History Series*.

Mikell was a leader in the movement to simplify and humanize criminal law and procedure. He published in 1915 the draft of a statute providing for simple forms of indictment. His critical study of the Penal Code of Pennsylvania, presented in an address delivered to the Law Association of Philadelphia, led to the appointment of a Commission to prepare a revision of this Code. Mikell was the Secretary and Draftsman of the Commission, which completed its work in 1922. While the revision was not adopted, he had demonstrated his skill as a legislative draftsman. When the American Law Institute decided in 1924 to prepare the draft of a Code of Criminal Procedure, he was appointed senior Reporter. He was well equipped for this

work. To an extensive knowledge of the subject acquired through long study he added clarity of thought and precision of statement. Though never opinionated he was firm in adhering to his well grounded convictions. One of his associates in the preparation of the Code wrote me: "His complete integrity and high-souled genuineness of thought and action made a deep impression upon me. And his accomplishments as a legal scholar and teacher rank him among the most notable figures of our profession."

Further valuable contributions to the work of the American Law Institute were made by him. In 1935 he presented, as Reporter, the draft of an act on Double Jeopardy and later he was an Adviser in the preparation of the Model Youth Correction Act. After his official retirement he continued to write and in 1942 published an article on "The Doctrine of Entrapment in the Federal Courts." For several years he was engaged in an intensive study of the problems of the mental element in crime. Unfortunately for those interested in this subject the work was not completed.

Mikell was temperamentally well fitted for administrative work although he had no great enthusiasm for it. Always courteous and patient, he was at the same time firm in his stand when a matter of principle was involved. Throughout his administration, which covered the difficult periods of the First World War and the expansive era of the late twenties, he never swerved in his maintenance of high standards for the admission and graduation of students. While details were distasteful to him, he never neglected them. He was not impulsive nor did he permit himself to be hurried in making a decision. His official relations with the other members of the faculty were marked to an exceptional degree by a harmony of respect and friendship. He was always accessible to students and never spared time or effort in assisting them.

My personal relations with Will Mikell were based on an intimate friendship which began some years before I became his colleague in 1915. He was a delightful companion. In conversation he combined subtle humor with a wit that was always sprightly and sometimes even playful. Ordinarily men become more conservative in their opinions as they grow older. This was not true of Will Mikell, for he was always ready to accept new ideas which his reason approved, and his attitude toward public and social problems became increasingly liberal. He had a great capacity for enjoyment. Reading of fiction was his chief diversion, but he also liked games—golf, billiards, bridge —and played them well. Simply to be alive was for him a pleasure and he resented as wasted the hours spent in sleep.

HISTORIC 96 YEAR OLD KAO BADGE FOUND©

History and tradition are ingrained in the Kappa Alpha Order. The story of Brother John Perryclear Scoville and his badge highlights an interesting chapter in Kappa Alpha lore. The story begins in the fall of 1917, when John Perryclear Scoville of Orangeburg, South Carolina enrolled at The Citadel. John was a slight young man, five foot six inches tall and weighing 135 lbs., but he took to the rigorous cadet life and even made it onto the Citadel football and baseball teams. In those days, the several hundred member Corps of Cadets needed anyone interested, no matter their size, to flesh out a small football team playing that relatively new sport. The Citadel had first started fielding a football team in 1905.

By the fall of 1919, John Scoville was a junior cadet majoring in physics and playing second string right end on the varsity football squad. On November 27, 1919, the squad travelled to Columbia to play the vaunted University of South Carolina in what had become an intense, annual, Thanksgiving rivalry. Since their first game in 1907, the two schools had played each other 12 times, with USC winning seven times, and The Citadel winning three times and there were two tied games.

In those days, football was mostly a game of "three yards and a cloud of dust". Pass plays were rare and there was no such thing as a "wide receiver". Most games were boring affairs with low scores. Such was the game played on November 27, 1919 and near the end of the third quarter, the game was tied at 7-7.

Spratt Moore was the Citadel quarterback. The Citadel had a huge player by the name of Captain Crouch, who played both fullback and first string right end. Because of his size, Crouch did most of the Citadel

scoring with the help of Moore. Crouch and Moore, taking turns running the ball, got it down to the USC 20 yard line. There they were stopped by the strong Carolina defense. Two running plays yielded only three yards, so it was third down and seven on the Carolina 13.

It was crunch time. On the next play.the five foot, six inch Scoville slipped behind the USC backfield and quarterback Moore threw a desperation "Hail Mary" pass to him on the one yard line. Scoville caught it and galloped into the end zone to score. His touchdown gave the Citadel the win, 14-7. The State newspaper the next day carried the headline, "Old Man Jinx was wearing a Citadel Uniform".

Badge #4652

John Scoville got credit for winning the game and his skill in catching the pass and beating the mighty "Gamecocks" made him a hero to the Corps of Cadets. Perhaps that is why, just six months later he was invited to join Kappa Alpha Order. Between 1883 and 1890, Theta Chapter of KAO operated clandestinely at The Citadel. In 1890, the college's governing board strictly banned all social fraternities and Theta Chapter went out of existence.

Thirty years later, in 1920, Beta Gamma chapter at the College of Charleston initiated a select, small group of Citadel cadets into the Order. John (Johnny) Perryclear Scoville was one of seven cadets initiated on May 7, 1920. He was awarded a KAO pin with Badge number 4652, and he and the other initiated men were registered by the Order as part of the old Theta Chapter.

Cadet Scoville would likely have been expelled from The Citadel had

the school learned he had joined a social fraternity, so he kept it a secret. In 1921, he graduated from The Citadel, worked for several road contractors as an asphalt chemist, and later became Maintenance Superintendent for the South Carolina Highway department in Barnwell County. He married Annie Mabry from Abbeville, S.C. The KAO badge was locked in a safe deposit box and over the years he never discussed with his wife or children his link to Kappa Alpha. His two sons later graduated from The Citadel. Both were totally unaware of their fathers' relationship with Kappa Alpha Order.

John P. Scoville, Jr. holding his father's historic badge

When John Perryclear Scoville died on April 18, 1967, his wife took control of the safe deposit box. Upon her death on February 15, 1999, the contents of the box were given to the oldest son, John Perryclear Scoville, Jr. a 1960 Citadel graduate. He noticed the small KA badge, but did not know what it was or what his father's connection was to it. It was some years later, in 2014, that he learned about the Theta Commission, its history and the significance of badge 4652. Today, John Perryclear Scoville, Jr. is a proud member of Theta Commission,

Appendix - Memoriabilia

the lineal descendant of Theta Chapter to which his father belonged.

Today, some 96 years after its issuance, efforts are underway to create a permanent, public display of this badge at The Citadel. This historic badge represents a material link between the athletic courage of a scrappy young man, and the storied traditions of Kappa Alpha Order and The Citadel.

©Thomas D. Wise, Historian Emeritus, Theta Commission,
Kappa Alpha Order, Charleston, SC

Knights of the Order

BIBLIOGRAPHY

Authored Books

Bond, Oliver J., *The History of The Citadel*, Garrett and Massie Publishers, Richmond, Va. 1936, reprinted, Southern Historical Press, 275 West Broad Street, Greenville, S.C.29602, 1989.

Conrad, James Lee, *The Young Lions, Confederate Cadets at War.*, Stackpole Books, Mechanicsburg, PA, 17055, 1997.

Easterby, J.H., *A History of the College of Charleston*, Scribner Press, 1935

Scott, Gary Thomas, *The Kappa Alpha Order, 1865-1897,* Heritage Books, Inc. Westminister, Maryland, 1994, 2007.

Stern, Philip Van Doren, *Robert E. Lee, The Man and The Soldier*, Bonanza Books, New York, New York, 1963.

Thomas, Emory M., *Robert E. Lee, A Biography*; W.W. Norton & Co., New York, 1995.

Thomas, John Peyre, *History of the South Carolina Military Academy*, 1783-1892, Palmetto Bookworks, Columbia, SC 29211, 1991, reprint of Walker, Evans & Cogswell, Charleston, SC, 1893.

Edited Books

The Writings of Marion Salley, edited by Hugo S. Ackerman, Orangeburg County Historical and Genealogical Society, R.L. Bryan Co. 1970.

Knights of the Order

The Varlet of Kappa Alpha Order, edited by Matt V. Bonner, Eleventh Edition, Kappa Alpha Order National Administrative Office, Lexington, VA.

History and Catalogue of the Kappa Alpha Fraternity, 1891, Chick, Joseph S., editor, Nashville, TN. Google, e-book.

Other Sources

Kappa Alpha Order, Theta Second Chapter, South Carolina Military Academy, p.267-271, (provided by Kappa Alpha Administrative Office, Lexington)

Directory of the Kappa Alpha Order 1865-1922, edited by W.B. Crawford, Orlando, FL.

General Catalogue of the Kappa Alpha Order, 1865-1900. No author.

Directory of the Kappa Alpha Order, 1865-1929, Edited by W. B. Crawford, Orlando, FL.

University of Pennsylvania Law Review, Volume 92, No. 3, 1944. William D. Lewis.

Alumni News, The Citadel, Spring-Summer, 2013. Published by The Citadel Alumni Association.

Index

Knights of the Order

Appendix - Index

Knights of the Order

Appendix - Index

Knights of the Order

Knights of the Order

ABOUT THE AUTHOR

Thomas Dewey Wise attended The Citadel for two years before transferring to the University of South Carolina where he received his Bachelor of Arts and Juris Doctor degrees. He later earned a Master of Laws degree from George Washington University. After being admitted to the South Carolina Bar, he entered the United States Army as a member of the Judge Advocate Generals Corps and volunteered for service in the 101st Airborne Division. After infantry officer and airborne schools, he served in Viet Nam where he was awarded the Bronze Star among other decorations. He returned to South Carolina after his military service and served as Assistant County Attorney before being elected to the South Carolina State Senate in 1972. Wise served in the State Senate for twelve years and served eight years on The Citadel Board of Visitors. In 2012, South Carolina Governor Nikki Haley awarded him the Order of the Palmetto, the state's highest civilian honor. He is a member of the Graves Province Court of Honor of Kappa Alpha Order. Dewey and his wife, Pat, live on Fenwick Island in Colleton County, S.C.

Knights of the Order

www.ingramcontent.com/pod-product-compliance
Lightning Source LLC
Chambersburg PA
CBHW060300100426
42742CB00011B/1816